W9-BSM-975

3 Dimensional Design

by
Katie Pasquini

Cover photography by William Burlingham, Chicago, Illinois
Inside photography by Lindsay Olsen, Eureka, California
Technical drawings by Katie Pasquini, Grass Valley, California
Illustrations by Chris Pasquini, Laporte, Colorado

Published by:
C & T Publishing
P.O. Box 1456
Lafayette, California
94549

ISBN 0-914881-19-1

Copyright © 1988 by Katie Pasquini

All rights reserved. No part of this book may be
reproduced in any form or by any means
without written permission from the publisher.

Library of Congress Catalog Card Number:
88- 70657

Manufactured in the United States of America.

Printed by Cal Central Press, Sacramento,
California

Editing by Randi Loft, Garberville, California

To:

J♪

I would like to thank a few important people, without whom this book would not have been as much fun to complete:

Debbie Thompson: For listening, and listening........
Dupree: For taking me on walks and making me laugh.
Moneca Calvert: who's only a phone call away
Randi Loft: the best friend anyone could ever hope for
Margaret Frazier: the little beeper
Eileen Mcgaff: the Barbecue Queen
The Blues Commandos: For their music.
To all the ladies from the guild who tried out the lessons prior to printing
Lindsay Olsen: For his wonderful photos of my quilts
Bill Burlingham: For his excellence in creating the cover of this book
Mike Spencer: the one-tun-won-ton man
Chris and Susie and Barrett: For all their help and support
J. Wood: For helping me become the 3 dimensional person that I am
The Coombs Clan: my second family in Seattle

I love you all, Thank-you!

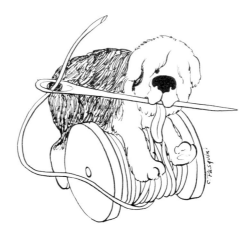

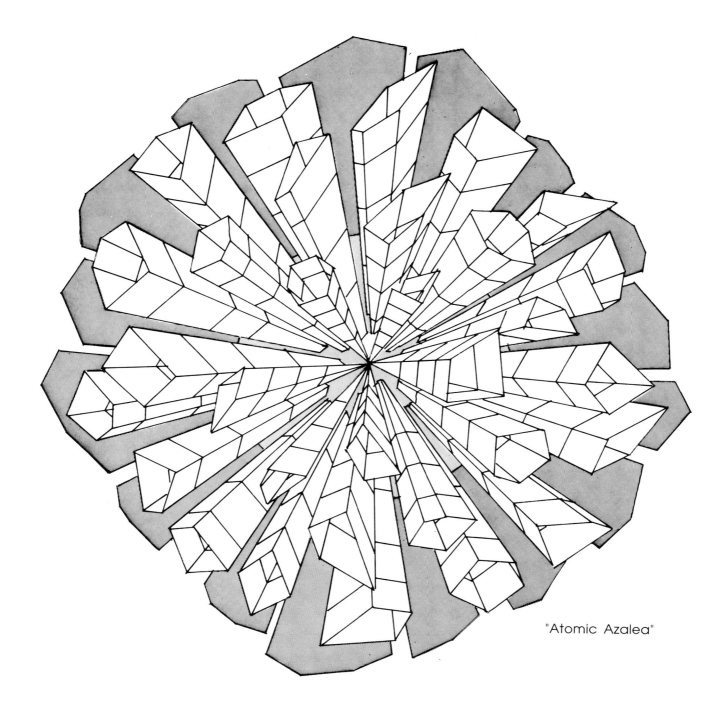

"Atomic Azalea"

FOREWORD ......

Welcome to the third dimension, or at least my view of the third dimension. My knowledge of three dimensional drawing came from the need to express my ideas or visualizations in my quilts. My art background began as a kid; I was always drawing. My parents encouraged each of their seven children to excel in whatever came natural. I was encouraged to take art classes, enjoying every moment of it. After finishing high-school, I felt it necessary to join the "real world" and go to work; however, I continued drawing and painting as a hobby.

Several years later, my father passed away and left a trust for each of us to continue schooling. Quitting work, I took art courses at the local junior college. I wish to thank him at this time for that gift. This schooling was interrupted in order for me to nurse my mother. During this time, I took a quilting class and became very interested in fabrics and quilting. In the past 10 years I have grown from the new quilter to the obsessed quilter. My style of design has gone from the traditional to the very modern. I began doing my own "thing" by designing Mandala quilts, (as seen in my book Mandala, 1984) using a center repeating triangle unit to create wall hangings. The last five years I have experimented with three dimensional designs on the flat quilt surface.

In my thirst for knowledge on the subject, I would haunt book stores for all sorts of books on three dimensional design. A lot of these were architecture books. Perusing these books, I would try to figure out how to reproduce an interesting drawing. Generally, the written word was incomprehensible to me; I would study the drawing, trace it, find the horizon, or the vanishing points, or any other references that would help me understand the drawing.

Two years ago I started teaching a workshop based on three dimensional drawing. Explaining my quilts and drawings, I gained a better understanding of how to draw perspectively. Now, I feel confident that I can explain to you how to add a third dimension to your quilts.

If you feel this is beyond you because of no art or drafting background, don't be put off; follow the lessons step-by-step and soon you can call yourself a draftsman, or a draftswoman if you prefer.

If you are experienced in this kind of work, then use the lessons to refresh your memory or, possibly, learn a different technique of achieving the same end.

In any case, enjoy and create!

Visualize yourself sitting in a nice comfortable chair, with some pleasant music playing quietly in the background. All the kids, or pets, or husbands, or roommates, are all out enjoying themselves, leaving you this wonderful time and space. Do you find it hard to visualize this scene? Try again!

You will be asked to visualize or imagine many things in the following pages; above is a nice fantasy to begin with!

This book is about three dimensional design, how to draw in perspective. Perspective is drawing things as you REALLY see them, not as you know them to be. When small, we drew as we really saw things. As we started school, we were soon taught to do things 'right', pushing our inner artistic ability further back in our subconscious. With this book, I hope to help you revitalize that unique ability to "see".

The most common mistake in learning to draw is putting pencil to paper before you have seen what you wish to draw, before visualizing. This technique of visualizing is important in perspective drawing. At the beginning of each lesson you will be asked to visualize what I wish drawn. It will help to read the image I want you to see, then close your eyes and "see" it. Follow the step-by-step instructions and actually put this image on paper. If you find the instructions difficult, stop and visualize the exercise again, making sure you are seeing all the parts.

Specific sizes and lengths will be stated in most of the lessons; please use these measurements the first time you try a lesson. Using the same measurements makes it easier to check the accuracy of each step. After you understand the concept, any measurement will fit the formula.

If you get a wonderful idea from any lesson, be sure to explore it. I have by no means covered every possibility. Finish the lesson so you understand the concept, then take it further; your idea may not be easy to reproduce at this time, but try to sketch it anyway. Then, when you complete the book, go back to the sketch, and with your accumulated knowledge, draw it easily.

Having the proper tools is very important in drafting. Improper tools can cause inaccuracies, resulting in frustration, (and when you are frustrated you have stopped having fun). Below is a list of drafting tools you should have to enjoy doing the lessons:

Pencils: any pencil will do; the most important thing is it remains sharp.

Compass: a Bow Compass with a rotating adjustment wheel.

Protractor: the best size protractor has about a 3" radius; try and find one that has an "x" at the center reference instead of a hole.

Graph Paper: is used to set up lessons; purchase by the sheet at art supply stores.

Eraser: SMALL (like the one on the end of your pencil).

Proportional Scale: used for enlarging or reducing drawings (See the lesson on Proportional scales to see how to use one).

Tracing Paper: 14" x 17" pad
I draw everything on tracing paper. I start an idea; then, thinking of something else to add to the image, I try it on a second piece of tracing paper laid over the original drawing. If I don't like what I see, I can remove the paper and try again. This way, what I like is not ruined. Some ideas may take many pieces of tracing paper to satisfy the image, so have plenty on hand.

Ruler: a transparent rule with an accurate grid marked on it.
This tool can't be praised enough; with each lesson you will be constantly making parallel lines. Such lines become an easy task with the grid ruler: place one of the lines of the ruler on top of a drawn line. Once the lines are identical, any other line drawn on the edge of the rule will be parallel.

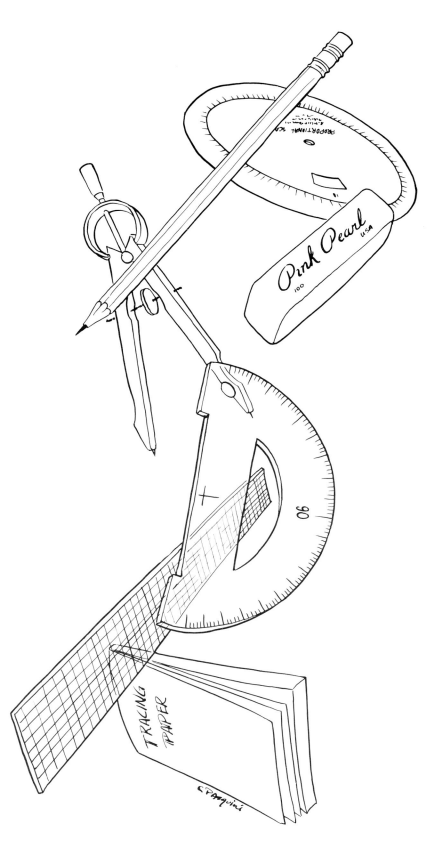

VANISHING POINTS..

Imagine standing on the road looking towards the horizon. The two sides of the road are parallel lines. What do you see? These lines appear to converge on the horizon, to a point called the "Vanishing Point". (From now on referred to as the VP). All parallel lines, viewed in perspective, converge at a vanishing point. Explore this idea through the following exercises.

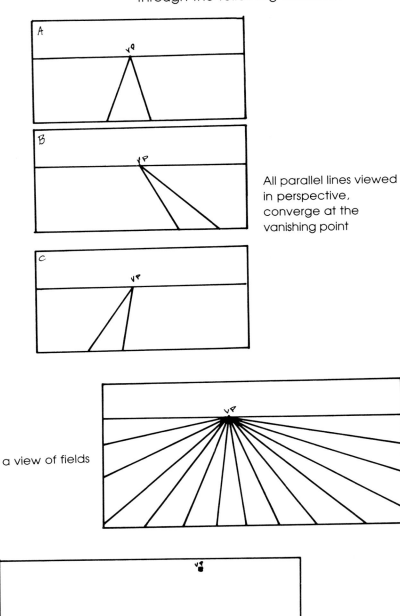

All parallel lines viewed in perspective, converge at the vanishing point

a view of fields

floor boards

use a protractor to create equal distances between the lines

Draw a rectangle approximately 3"x 5". Add a horizon line anywhere within the rectangle. Put a dot anywhere on the horizon line as your vanishing point. Now draw the two parallel lines of the road below the horizon in perspective. These lines will converge at your vanishing point. In drawing A, the viewer is standing in the middle of the road; in drawing B, to the left of the road; and, in drawing C, to the right. Remember, all parallel lines viewed in perspective, converge at the vanishing point.

Draw another 3" x 5" rectangle. Now you are in a field of vegetables. Draw a horizon line and VP in this rectangle. Using a ruler, draw any number of lines from the VP to the lower edge of the rectangle. The top section would be the sky and the lower section the field of vegetables.

Draw another rectangle with a horizon line. Place the VP above the horizon; it could even be outside of the rectangle. Line up your ruler with the VP and draw lines from the horizon to the lower edge of the paper. Do NOT draw the lines above the horizon line. This drawing could be boards of a deck or a floor.

Draw a rectangle with a horizon line, and a VP above the horizon line, in or out of the rectangle. In the previous drawings, spacing was not important. In this drawing, we want the lines to be equally spaced. This is done by using a protractor and marking equal distances. Place the protractor so the center reference is on top of the VP. Make a small mark every 5 or 10 degrees, depending on how close you want the lines to be.

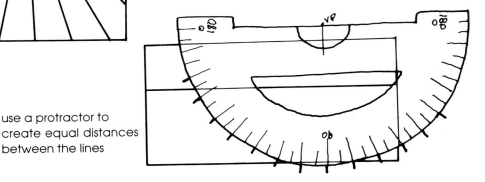

Connect the VP to the degree marks, drawing lines only within the ground area. This method divides an area into equal spaces.

Now, let's imagine the inside of a room, with paneling and floor boards. Draw a rectangle, with a horizon line. In this case, the horizon line would be where the wall and floor meet. Draw parallel lines, equal distance apart in the area representing the wall; this will be the panelling. Add a VP above the horizon line.

Add the floor boards by drawing lines relative to the VP from each corner of the wall boards, (the point where the wall lines meet the horizon line). Your drawing should now look like you imagined the room.

The placement of the vanishing point and horizon line determines where the viewer is standing. In the last illustration, the view is that of someone standing in the room. In the next illustration, the view is that of someone laying on the floor. Play with different vanishing points until you become comfortable with this theory.

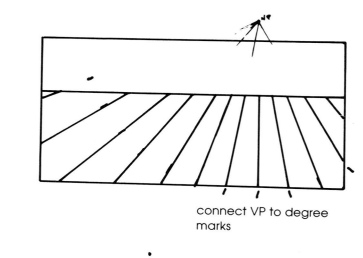

connect VP to degree marks

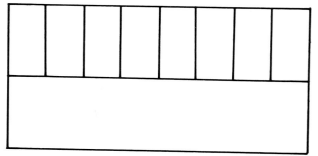

wall boards drawn equal distance

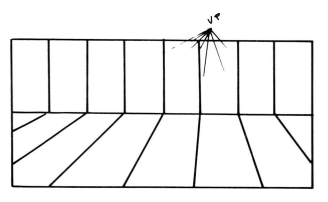

floor boards connected to wall

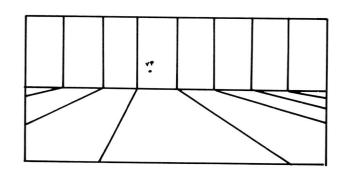

a lower view point

In this lesson, we will use one point perspective as a reference to draw a box. Visualize a cardboard box. Depending on your position, you will see different sides of this box, in combination or alone. Visualize yourself standing directly in front of the box at eye level. This is a frontal view of the box, and you will see only one surface. Now, lower the imaginary box. You, the viewer, are now higher than the box and can see two surfaces, the top and the front. Raise the box to eye level again, and turn it slightly to the right. Now you see two sides again, the front and right sides. Lowering the box again, you will see three surfaces of the box, the top, front and side. If this is difficult for you to imagine, do this exercise with an actual cardboard box.

There are several ways to draw a "box"; first, the simplest way:

Using graph paper under the tracing paper, draw a 2" square. Place the ruler from any two opposite corners. In order to see all sides of the box DO NOT put the vanishing point along this line; move the ruler slightly down and mark a vanishing point.

Very lightly, draw lines from the vanishing point to the 4 corners of the square. These lines create the 4 sides of the box.

Now we need to draw the back of the box. Begin by drawing the top of the back of the box parallel to top of the front of the box. Draw this line 1/2" from the front. Be sure this line is in between the two vanishing lines that come from the top corners of the box. Pivot the ruler on the edge of the line and draw the side of the box parallel to the front. Pivot from that edge and draw the bottom. The last line should connect and complete the back of the box. Remove the graph paper.

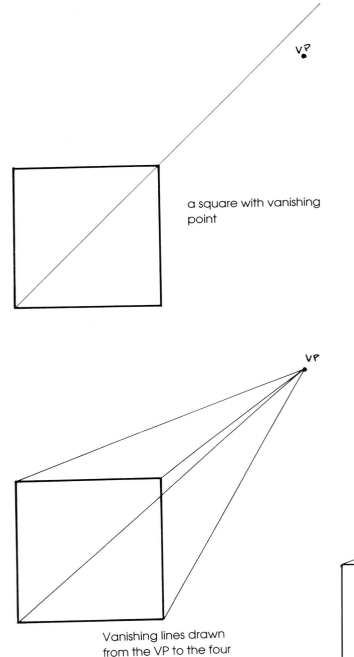

a square with vanishing point

Vanishing lines drawn from the VP to the four corners of the square.

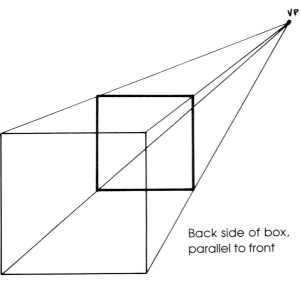

Back side of box, parallel to front

Darken the portion of the vanishing lines that are needed to create the box. This would be a transparent box, a box made of glass, or one made of poles. If you like, trace this transparent box without the vanishing lines.

Using a second piece of tracing paper, trace four boxes from the original box:

1. A solid box. Trace the original square, the top and the right side.

2. A box open at the top: Trace a solid box, then visualize the top of the box being open; the line that distinguishes the back edge will now show.

3. A box open at the side: Again draw a solid box but with the side gone; the line that determines the back bottom will now be seen.

4. A box open at the front: Draw a solid box with a missing front side; draw all the lines that let you see the inside.

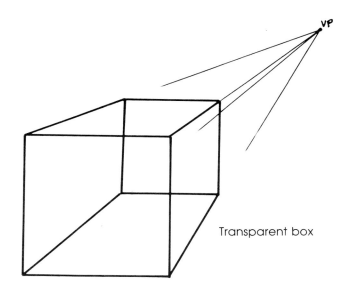

Transparent box

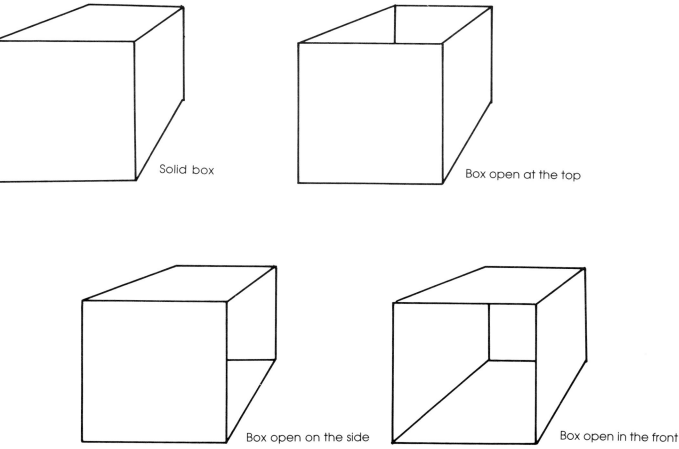

Solid box

Box open at the top

Box open on the side

Box open in the front

ONE POINT WALLS..

In this lesson, we will use one point perspective to create walls or units that seem to come toward the viewer. Imagine that you are standing at the edge of a brick wall. Imagine another brick wall placed against this wall, only closer.

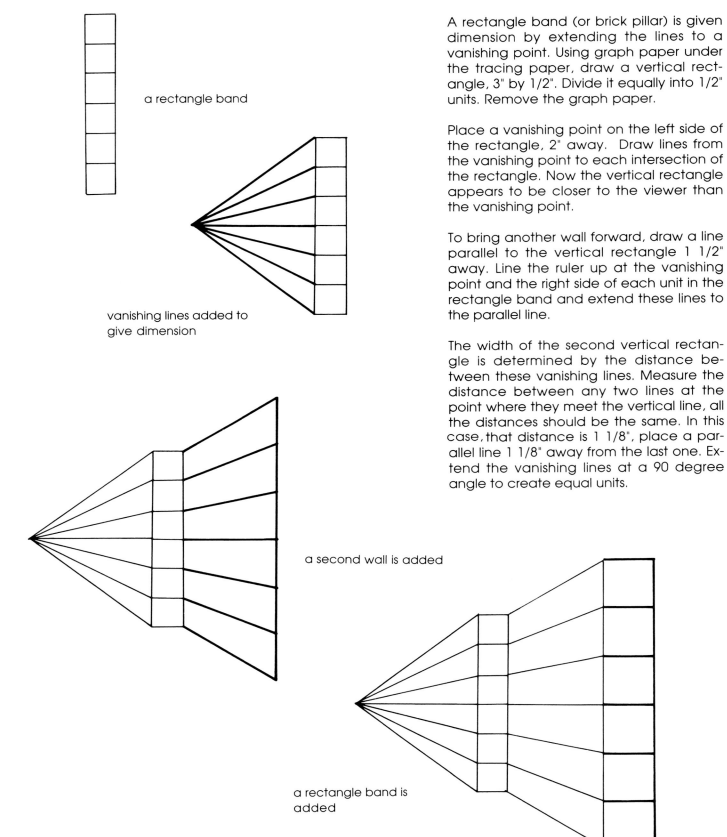

a rectangle band

vanishing lines added to
give dimension

a second wall is added

a rectangle band is
added

A rectangle band (or brick pillar) is given dimension by extending the lines to a vanishing point. Using graph paper under the tracing paper, draw a vertical rectangle, 3" by 1/2". Divide it equally into 1/2" units. Remove the graph paper.

Place a vanishing point on the left side of the rectangle, 2" away. Draw lines from the vanishing point to each intersection of the rectangle. Now the vertical rectangle appears to be closer to the viewer than the vanishing point.

To bring another wall forward, draw a line parallel to the vertical rectangle 1 1/2" away. Line the ruler up at the vanishing point and the right side of each unit in the rectangle band and extend these lines to the parallel line.

The width of the second vertical rectangle is determined by the distance between these vanishing lines. Measure the distance between any two lines at the point where they meet the vertical line, all the distances should be the same. In this case, that distance is 1 1/8", place a parallel line 1 1/8" away from the last one. Extend the vanishing lines at a 90 degree angle to create equal units.

This process can be repeated over and over again to create as many units coming forward as you wish.

If you turn your paper the walls will appear as a frontal view of steps!

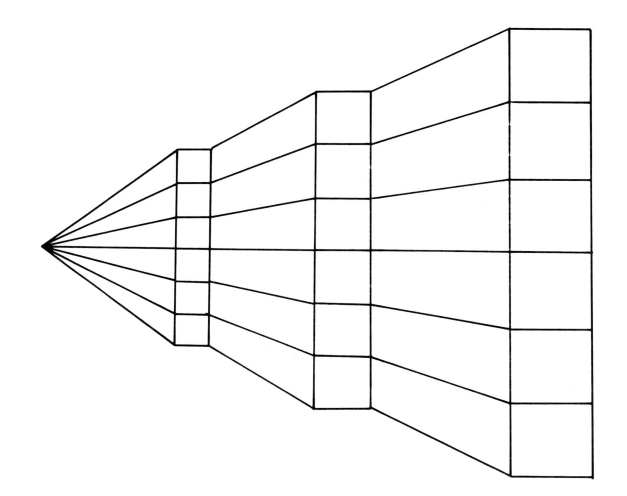

Visualize a set of steps. First picture these steps from the side; notice how the lines of the steps vanish away from you.

To draw steps, begin by drawing the flats and the rises. With tracing paper over graph paper, draw one inch steps (four of these should be enough).

Place a VP to the right above the top step and beyond the bottom step. Draw vanishing lines from each corner of the steps to the VP. Draw these lines lightly as you will not need the entire line.

NOTE: This also looks like an open fan!

To define the back side of the steps, draw a line parallel to the front of the steps between the same set of vanishing lines. Line up the grid ruler so the one inch line is on the center step and draw a parallel line. Pivot the ruler at the corner, matching the line and draw a parallel line. (Only the first line is measured depending on the length of the step you want; the rest of the lines are determined by the intersection of the parallel line and the vanishing line). Continue pivoting up and down until the steps are complete. These lines must be drawn in order; do not draw all of the horizontal lines then all the vertical lines. One line pivots off the previous line.

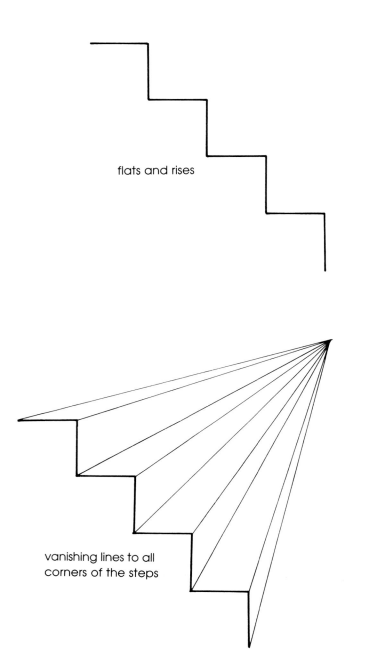

flats and rises

vanishing lines to all corners of the steps

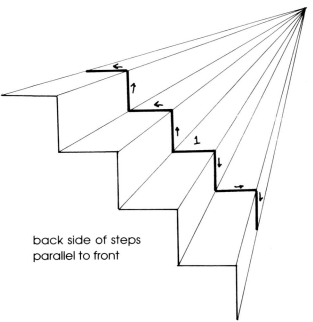

back side of steps parallel to front

Darken the lines that complete the steps and add a line at the bottom and the side to make solid steps. Now your steps are complete.

Lets open up the area under the steps to add more dimension. Draw a triangle that fills the space beneath the steps. Draw a light vanishing line from the corner of the triangle to the VP.

To find the back of the triangle, you also need to find the back top and bottom of the steps. These two points are indicated with arrows. Line your ruler up at these points and draw a parallel line within the triangle to the vanishing line. If your steps were drawn true, then these two lines should meet at the vanishing line. If not, try again, being more accurate in your original steps. Darken the portion of the vanishing line that is part of the steps.

To complete the lesson, retrace the steps omitting the unnecessary vanishing lines.

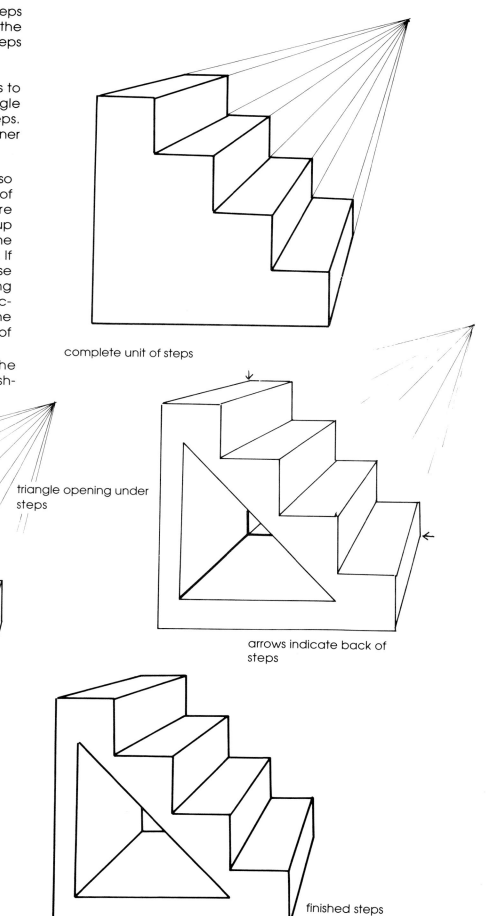

complete unit of steps

triangle opening under steps

arrows indicate back of steps

finished steps

Lets imagine we're standing at one end of a paneled wall. The board closest to you is the largest, and, as each board gets farther away it appears to get smaller and smaller, in width, and height. This is perspective.

Start by lightly drawing a horizon line. Now draw a 4" line perpendicular to the horizon line on the left side of the line. This perpendicular line is the edge of the wall that is closest to the viewer. Place a VP on the horizon line about 8" from the perpendicular line. From the vanishing point, draw two lines to each end of the perpendicular line. End the wall by placing a line 5" away from and parallel to the perpendicular line. Label both perpendicular lines A. We now have a wall that is a rectangle in perspective.

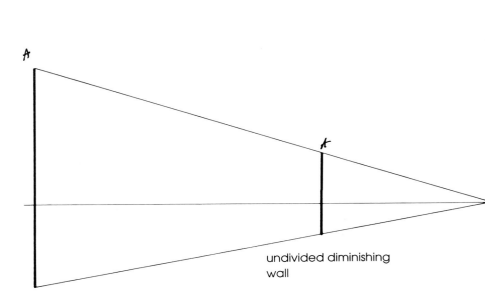

undivided diminishing wall

Now, we will divide the rectangle into equal units. The easiest way to divide a rectangle in half is by making an x from corner to corner, and placing a line parallel to the two sides where the x intersects. It may be helpful to also draw this wall from the frontal view. Draw a rectangle 1" x 2" to represent the frontal wall. Label the two vertical, parallel lines A. Divide this rectangle in half using a lightly drawn x. Label the center line B.

The same principle is applied to divide the perspectively correct wall in half. Draw an x from corner to corner, adding a vertical line at the intersection, parallel to the two sides. This line is the center of the wall. Label this line B.

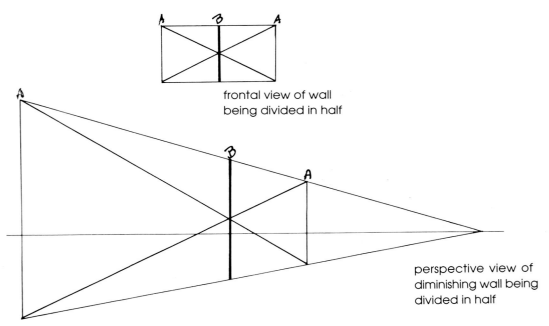

frontal view of wall being divided in half

perspective view of diminishing wall being divided in half

To divide the wall into smaller units continue the same process. Now there are two units each needing to be divided in two. On either side of B, an x is placed from corner to corner: AB and BA; where the x crosses add parallel lines. Label these two new lines C.

Then place an x in each of these sections to divide the wall once again, adding parallel lines where each of these cross. The first x is between line AC; the next between CB, then BC, and lastly, CA.

IMPORTANT---Remember, each time the wall is divided it must be done equally. Each unit must be divided the same; any unit left undivided will throw off the perspective.

With so many lines, confusion may be avoided by using colored pencils to do each of the steps. Make the B divisions in one color, the C divisions in another, and so on.

To finish the wall, place a piece of tracing paper over the drawing and trace only the lines that are needed to create the illusion (not the crosses).

This method can be used to divide any surface that recedes or diminishes from the viewer, whether it is a wall, floor, or a side of a box.

NOTE: Before the drawing was retraced, it was full of various shapes created by the intersecting of the vertical wall lines and the diagonal lines. This gives a wonderful excuse to change fabrics and color choices and could add more interest to a diminishing wall in a quilted piece.

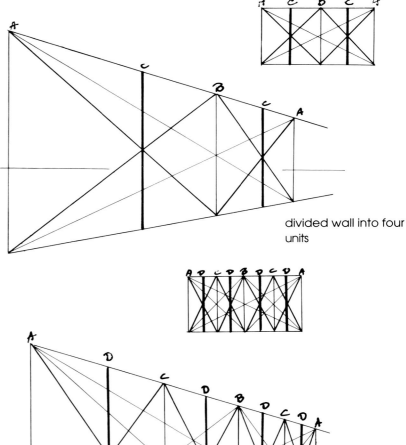

divided wall into four units

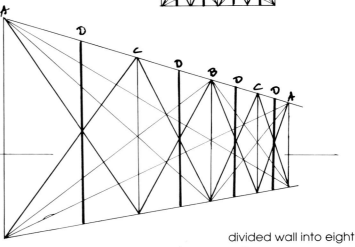

divided wall into eight units

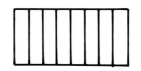

complete diminishing wall

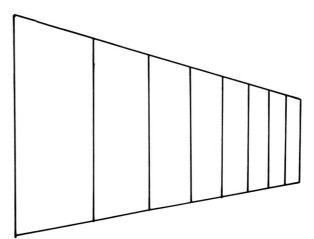

We have drawn a box with one point perspective; it can also be drawn using two point perspective. This method can create a rather distorted and interesting box. These "boxes" can give the illusion of being very large, like skyscrapers. Imagine you are looking out the window from the 30th floor at a 100 story building. It will not look like the cardboard box. Say you are still on the 30th floor looking at a two story warehouse. How would that look? Now imagine you are on the sidewalk across the street looking up at that 100 story building.

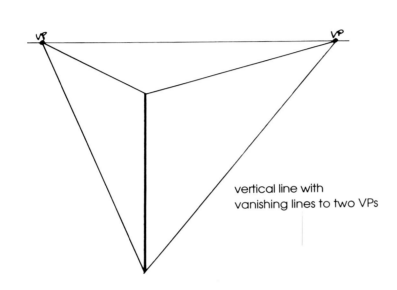

vertical line with vanishing lines to two VPs

How would you draw these "boxes"? One way is to use two vanishing points (2 point perspective).

Draw a horizon line. Now draw a dark vertical line, 3" long, below the horizon line; this will be the front corner of the box. Place two vanishing points on either side of this line on the horizon line. Place these VP's between 2" and 3" from the original line. Draw very light vanishing lines from each end of the center line to the VP.

Place a dark parallel line on either side of the vertical line, any distance you chose inside the vanishing points. You have made the right and left side of the box. Be sure that these two new lines are parallel to the original vertical line.

From the VP on the right, lightly draw two lines to both ends of the parallel line on the left front corner. From the left VP, lightly draw two lines to the right parallel line. There may seem to be too many lines, and finding a box in this mess may seem impossible! Follow the next steps to help you find your "box".

two parallel lines to designate the back edge of the box

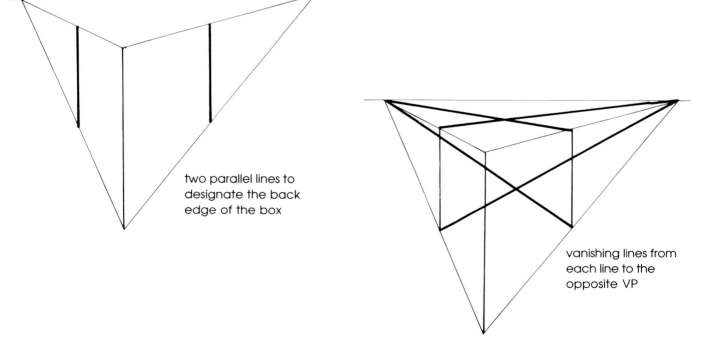

vanishing lines from each line to the opposite VP

The three vertical lines are the corners of the box. Think of these lines as being made out of steel. They cannot be erased or altered in any way. Draw these lines in very dark. These will be referred to as steel lines from now on.

To find the box in all of these lines, start with your pencil at the top of the center steel line. Follow that line to the bottom. Pivot left or right and follow that line until you reach another steel line. Pivot and go up that steel line to the top. Turn again, following that line to the top of the center steel line. This is one front side of your box. To find the other side, follow the same steps, pivoting at the bottom of the center steel line in the opposite direction.

Now you need to find the top of the box. Place your pencil at the top of the left steel line; follow the line that goes up and to the right. This line will be crossed by another vanishing line; pivot and follow that line to the right steel line. There is the top of your box.

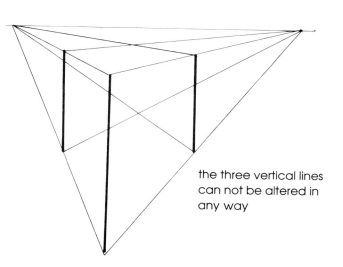

the three vertical lines can not be altered in any way

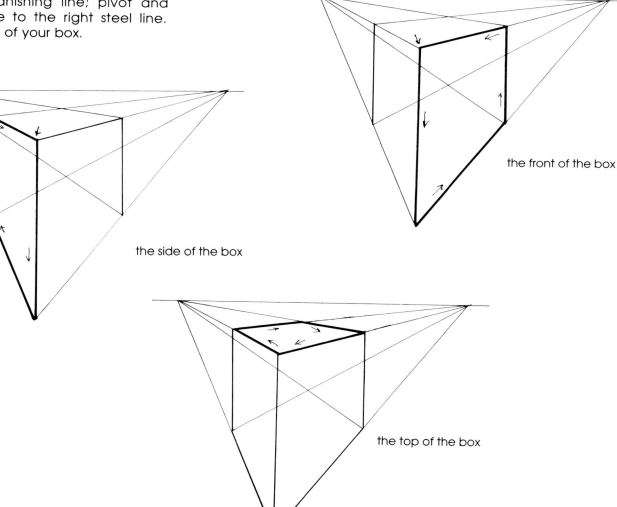

the side of the box

the front of the box

the top of the box

BOX - TWO POINT ....

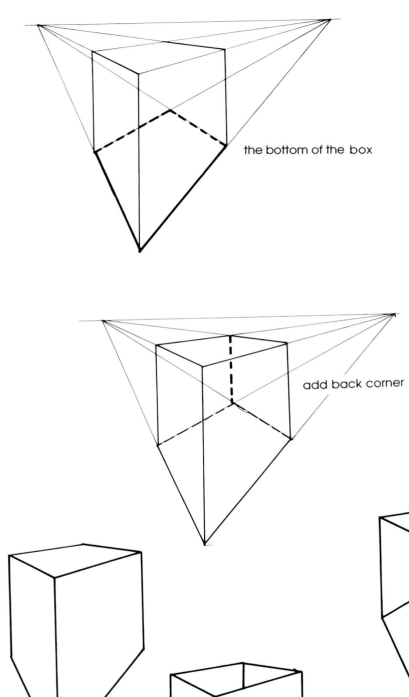

the bottom of the box

The bottom of the box is found in the same manner. Place your pencil at the bottom of the left steel line and follow the vanishing line up and to the right. That line will be crossed by another vanishing line; pivot and follow that line down to the right steel line. That is the bottom of your box. It may be easier to see if this line is drawn as a broken line.

There is one line missing, the back corner of the box. A vertical line parallel to the other three is added where the two sets of vanishing lines cross.

Using a second piece of tracing paper, trace four more boxes based on the original; (as we did in the one point perspective lesson) a solid box, a box open at the top, one open at the side, and one open in the front.

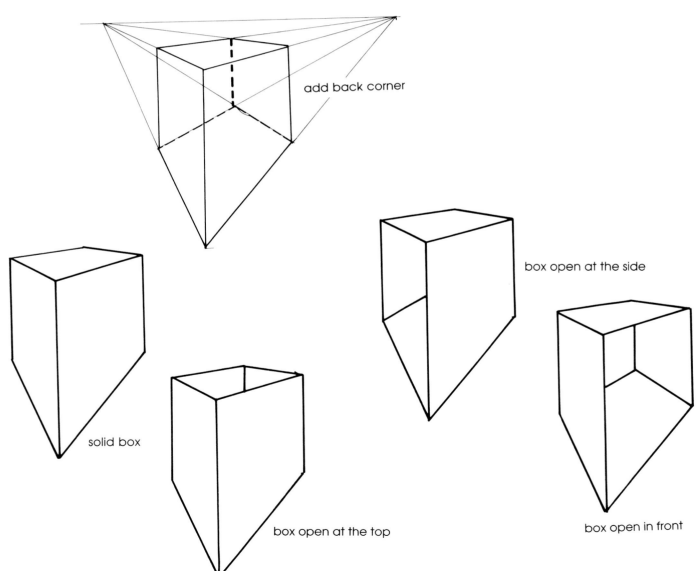

add back corner

box open at the side

solid box

box open at the top

box open in front

Many interesting "buildings" or boxes can be created by placing the two vanishing points, or "points of perspective", in different positions on the horizon line.

To get a lower building, like a large warehouse, the first line is shorter and the two VP's are placed further from that line.

A taller building is achieved by making the original line longer and the two VP's lower and closer to that line.

You can make these "boxes" float in space by lowering the horizon line and the VP's even farther to expose the bottom of the box.

Once you have played with all the different possibilities, it may be fun to do the exercises from the previous box lesson. Open these boxes on the top or side, or make them solid. Here are some possibilities:

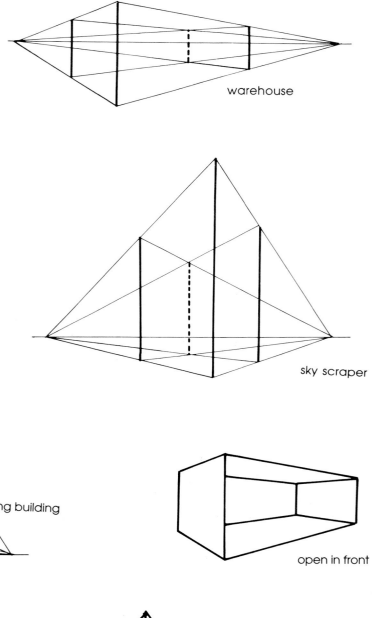

warehouse

sky scraper

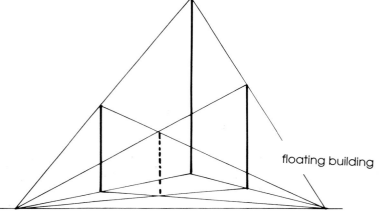

floating building

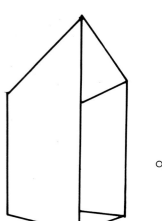

open in front

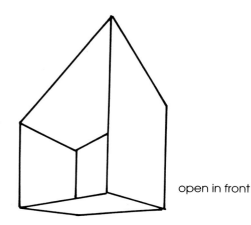

open in front

open at side

Imagine seeing different floors in these buildings, or shelves in the boxes.

Let's try one simplified example. Using the 2 VP's, draw a very tall building or box.

Trace your box so that it is open on one side.

To add a floor or a shelf, place a line on the left inside wall. The positioning of this line is determined by the vanishing point opposite that wall, the VP on the right.

Then, using the other vanishing point, the one on the left, draw lines that define the shelf. The possibilities go on and on. Think of something, visualize it, then draw what your mind sees.

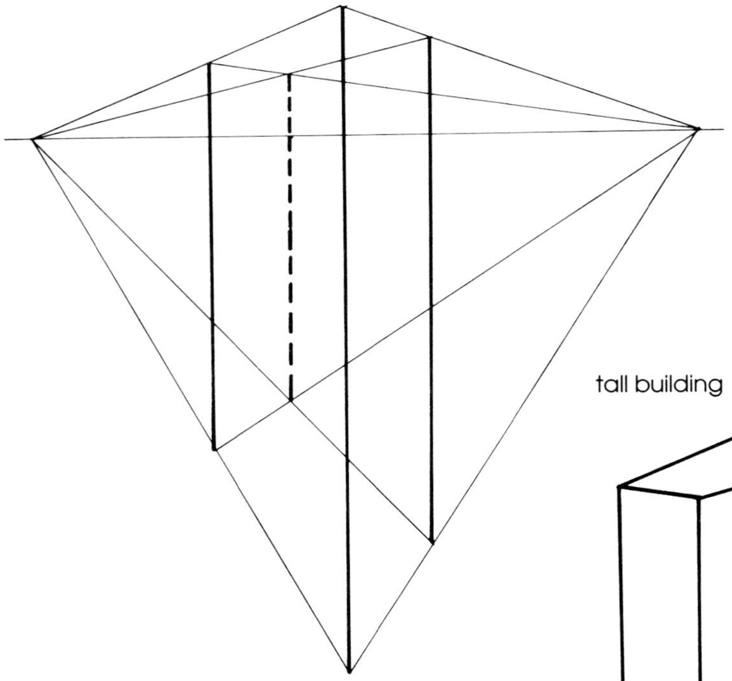

tall building

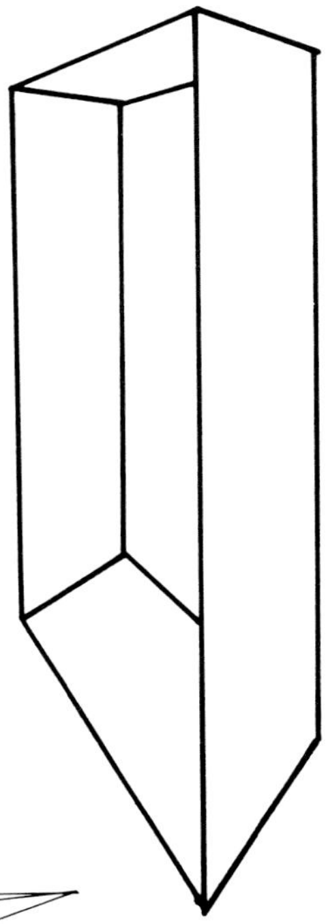

open at the side

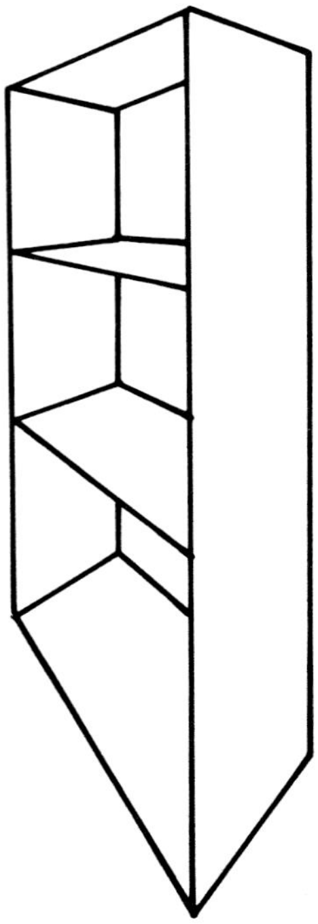

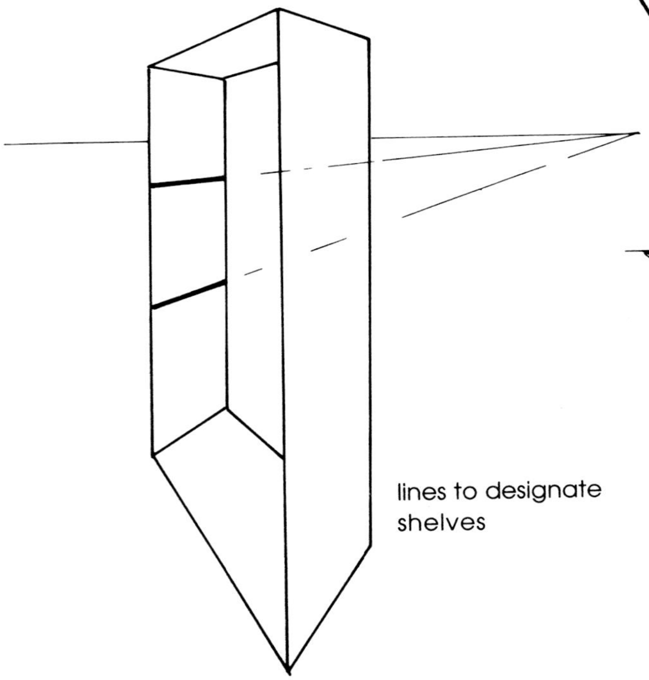

lines to designate shelves

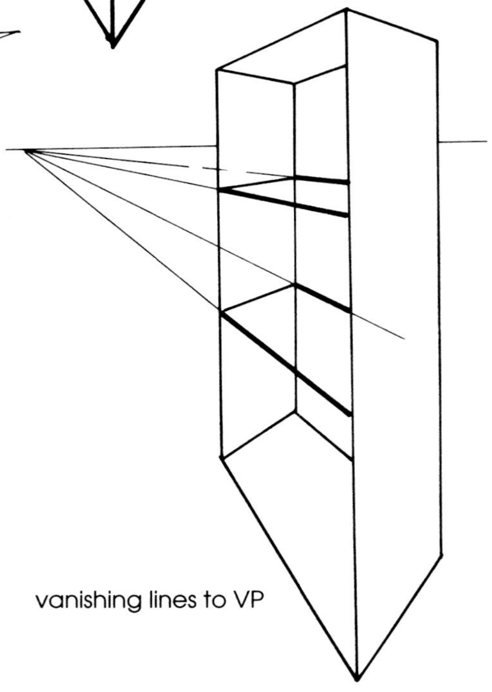

vanishing lines to VP

box with shelves

Imagine a vertical square, divide it in half. That was easy; just two diagonals from corner to corner. Divide each new square again, and again. You now have 64 little squares as a unit instead of one big square. This is how:

Draw a horizon line with a VP at one end. Add a perpendicular line; the length of this line is arbitrary. Draw vanishing lines from both ends of the perpendicular line to the VP. End the square with another perpendicular line. Find the center of this square with a set of diagonal lines. Through this vertex (the point where the diagonals cross), draw lines parallel to the sides. One will be vertical and one will go to the VP.

There are now four equal squares instead of one. Divide one of those squares in half by the same method; again, a set of diagonal lines. Through this new vertex draw lines parallel to the sides. One will be vertical and one will go to the VP.

Repeat the process one more time. This last little square is one 64th of the whole square.

Now divide the entire square using this method to end up with a vertical square divided into 64 smaller units.

Trace the square eliminating the diagonal lines.

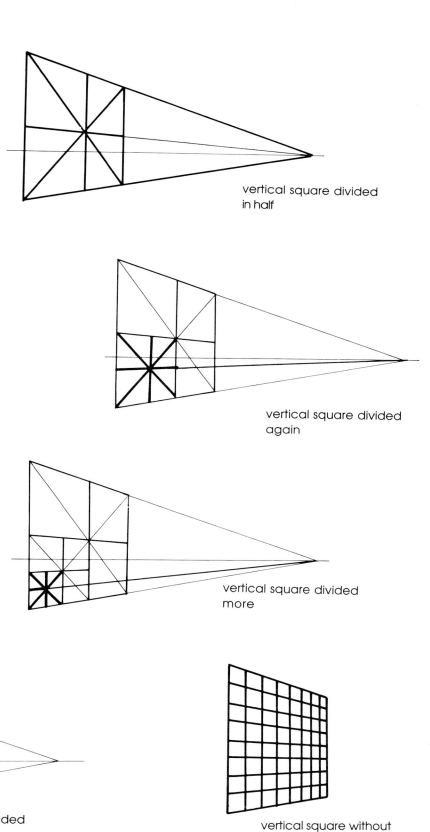

vertical square divided
in half

vertical square divided
again

vertical square divided
more

vertical square divided
into 64 equal units

vertical square without
lines of reference

Imagine a square. Find the center of the square by imagining diagonal lines from opposite corners. This center point will determine the placement of the center lines parallel to the sides. Draw a 2" square and its divisions. This will be considered the frontal view.

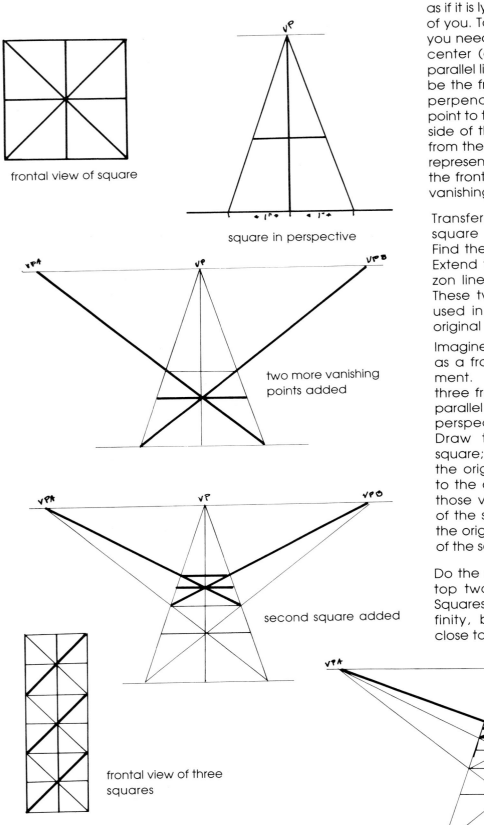

frontal view of square

square in perspective

two more vanishing points added

second square added

frontal view of three squares

Now imagine this square in perspective, as if it is lying on the ground directly in front of you. To draw this square in perspective, you need a horizon line with the VP in the center (one point perspective). Draw a parallel line 3" below the horizon line ; it will be the front side of your square. Place a perpendicular line from the vanishing point to the front line. Measure 1" on either side of the perpendicular line. Draw lines from the VP to these marks; draw a line to represent the top of the square 1 1/4" from the front of the square, between the two vanishing lines.

Transfer all the lines from the original square onto this perspective square. Find the center with two diagonal lines. Extend these diagonal lines to the horizon line and label them VPa and VPb. These two new vanishing points will be used in the next exercises. Darken the original square.

Imagine a row of three squares. Draw this as a frontal view using the 2" measurement. Notice the diagonal lines in the three frontal squares. The diagonals are parallel to one another. All parallel lines in perspective vanish to a common VP. Draw the diagonals of the second square; they begin at the top corners of the original perspective square and go to the opposite vanishing points. Where those vanishing lines cross is the center of the second square. Where they cross the original vanishing lines will be the top of the square. Draw this parallel line.

Do the exact same thing again using the top two corners of the second square. Squares can be drawn on like this into infinity, becoming much too small and close to see after a while.

third square added

Let's take this lesson a step further and do the same thing using a grouping of squares, nine squares, three by three (A Nine Patch). Draw a frontal view of a nine patch to orient yourself with the subject.

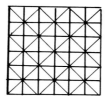

frontal view of nine squares

Trace the previous drawing of three squares in perspective, including all three VPs. We now need to add to both sides of this drawing to create our perspective nine patch. The length of the square is 2"; measure 2" on either side of the square. Connect these two points to the VP, extending the parallel lines that designate each square. Add missing diagonals and center parallels to complete the picture. Notice that all of these diagonals continue to match the opposite VPa or VPb.

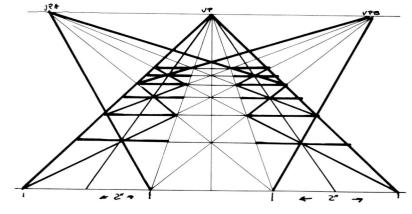

perspective view of nine squares

This information enables you to draft any pieced quilt block in one point perspective; let's try "Prairie Queen". Using tracing paper, draw this quilt block from the nine patch frontal view, tracing just the lines you need. To draw this in perspective, return to the nine patch in perspective and trace the same lines of Prairie Queen. Find each square and trace the proper lines. This can be done with any traditional block you choose!

frontal view of Prairie Queen quilt block

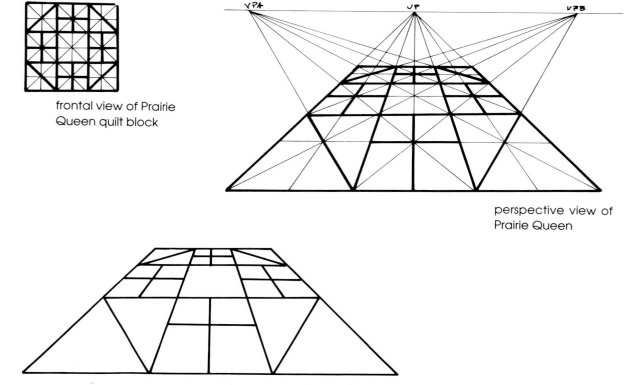

perspective view of Prairie Queen

Prairie Queen without reference line

Let's go even further with this idea! See how one thing leads to another when you let your mind play with these lessons! Go back to the drawing of the frontal nine squares. Picture three randomly place squares around the nine patch. Despite these additions, the pattern is still not very exciting. Let's see what happens when we draw it in perspective.

To add a square on the right, extend the bottom line 2", (the length of the square). Connect the end of the line to the VP. Locate the top line of the adjoining square and extend it to the vanishing line. That's the new square! Extend the center line and add the diagonals. Notice that these diagonals also meet at VPa and VPb.

The same process is followed to add the square on the top left. Darken the vanishing line from the top left corner of the existing squares to VPb; continue this line to the left of the squares. That is one diagonal of the new square. The other diagonal is already there; find that diagonal between the lower corner of the existing back square and VPa; darken it. Extend the top and bottom and center of the back row of squares. From the far left corner, draw a line to the original VP.

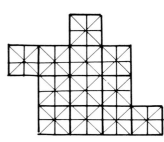

frontal view of random
grouping of squares

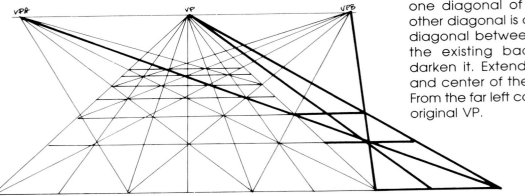

addition of right front
square

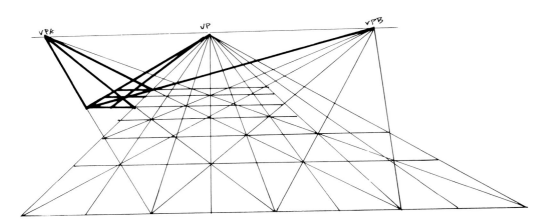

addition of left rear
square

And last, the little square at the top. All of the lines are already there except one, the top of the square. Place a parallel line between the center two diagonals and darken the lines needed.

To finish, trace just the lines that are in the frontal view, (none of the extending vanishing lines). Additional lines add depth to this drawing.

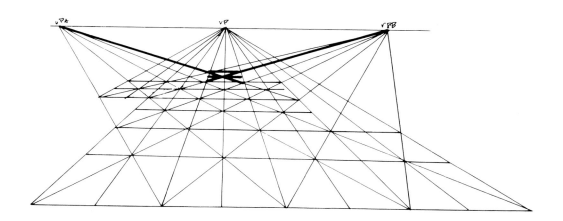

addition of back square

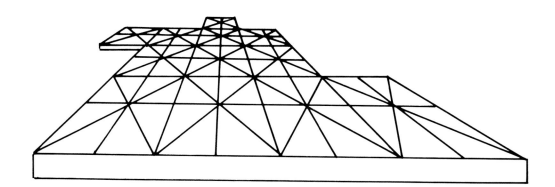

perspective squares

SPHERES..

Three dimensional spheres are spheres that look as if they could roll right off the page, or quilt. Imagine a ball; imagine a grid; imagine the grid on the ball. Another way to see this is to imagine a beach ball, the kind with the different colored sections.

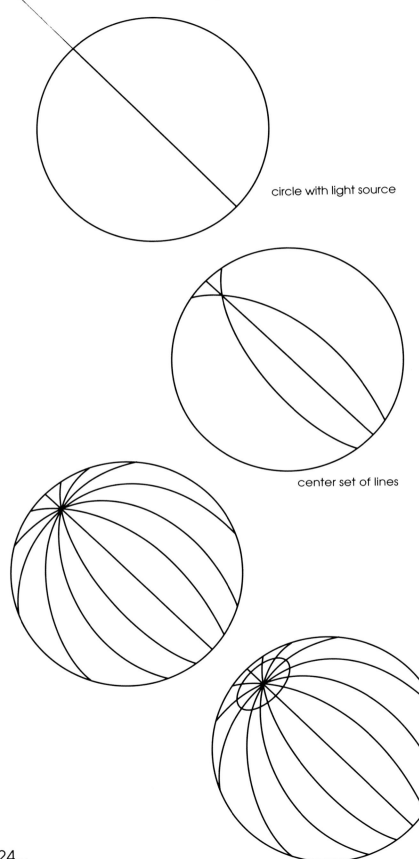

circle with light source

center set of lines

horizontal lines of circle are actually flattened circles

Begin by drawing a 3" circle with a compass. Note where the point of the compass was placed. Pick a light source, a point from which the light is coming. Using a ruler, draw a line through the center of the circle using the light source as the reference. This will be the only line that is drawn using a ruler. Near the top edge of the circle, make a mark on the line that will be called the "point of crossing". All vertical lines will cross at this point.

Remember to see this circle as a sphere and not as a flat circle on the paper. Draw lines that follow the curve of the sphere. To begin, draw a line on either side of the straight line. This line will be slightly curved. Imagine your pencil coming up from behind the ball, crossing the point of crossing and going down the front of the sphere. Do this on both sides of the straight line.

Now draw another set of lines; these lines will be slightly more curved than the first two. Continue adding lines, first one on one side then on the other, until you have filled the space; this will look like the beach ball. These are the vertical lines of the imagined grid.

The horizontal lines of the imagined grid are actually flattened circles. Using the point of crossing as the center, draw a flattened circle. Again, imagine this flat circle as a three dimensional sphere. It may help to circle your pencil around in the air a couple of times before you actually draw to help you get the feel.

Continue adding circles. After the first circle you will only be drawing a portion of the flattened circles because the rest will be behind the sphere.

Do not be discouraged if your first attempt is not exactly what you expected! It took many attempts before I got my first recognizable sphere. Here are some examples of what you may be doing wrong:

The first two lines are too curved. These lines are close to the center straight line so they must be similar to it and only slightly curved.

The circles are too round. You want to view these circles in perspective so they will be ellipses or flattened circles. Draw different sizes of circles, and place the light source differently until you are comfortable drawing spheres. Once you get a fairly good sphere, lay tracing paper on top of it and trace the good parts and change the bad.

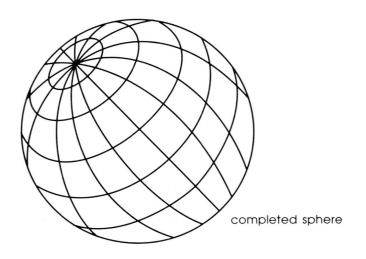

completed sphere

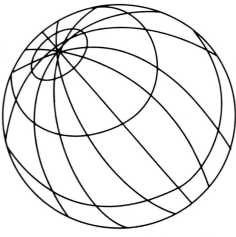

wrong: circles are too round

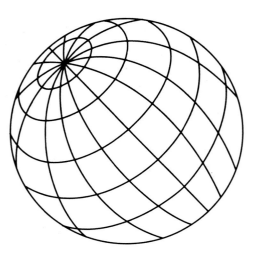

wrong: lines are too curved

Color Plates ....

The quilts on the next pages were all created from the lessons in this book. All of the quilts were machine pieced and hand quilted by Katie. Line and color combine to create the dimensional quality of each. They are shown in the order that they were made, showing you how each quilt leads to the next. A few of the later pieces contain hand reverse applique circles. The fiber content of each piece varies; lamé, a shiny fabric, was added to many pieces as an accent. Because all are wall hangings, the need for 100% cotton was dismissed.

"Too much discipline of temperament runs the danger of discouraging the spirit rather than leaving it happily free. Science is essentially intellectual; art is essentially emotional."

Faber Birren.

Plate 1 **MELANIE'S ROSE**   courtesy of the Perklo Collection

72" x 72" 1982   machine pieced, hand quilted
Diminishing circles and a transparent overlay effect were used to create this mandala
composition. A memorial piece to little Melanie Rose.

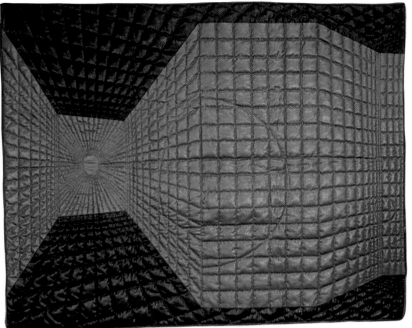

Plate 2 **IN SEARCH OF THE LOST CORD**
courtesy of Edward Stanton III

30" x 23" 1982 machine pieced, hand quilted, polished cotton.
Two vanishing points give dimension to this hand quilted wall hanging about searching for meanings to lifes injustices.

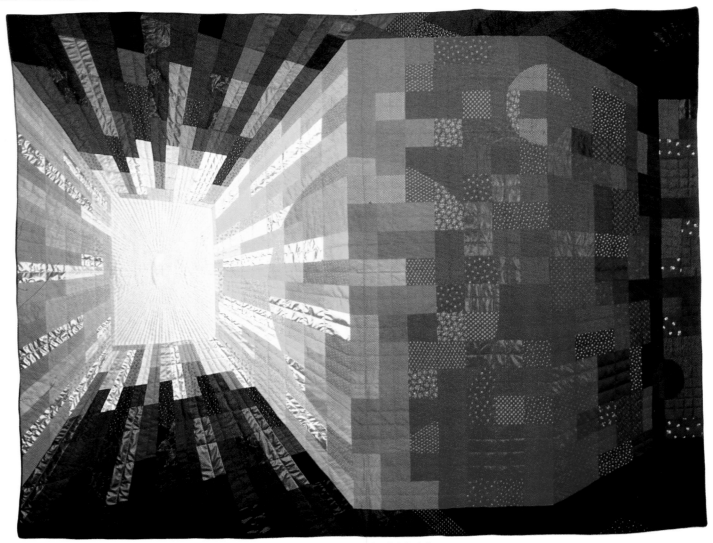

Plate 3 **THRESHOLD OF A DREAM**   courtesy of Gail Motsinger

80" x 72" 1982 machine pieced, hand quilted
A different interpretation of the original drawing (In Search of the Lost Cord) using colored fabrics. A bright happy quilt representing good times to come.

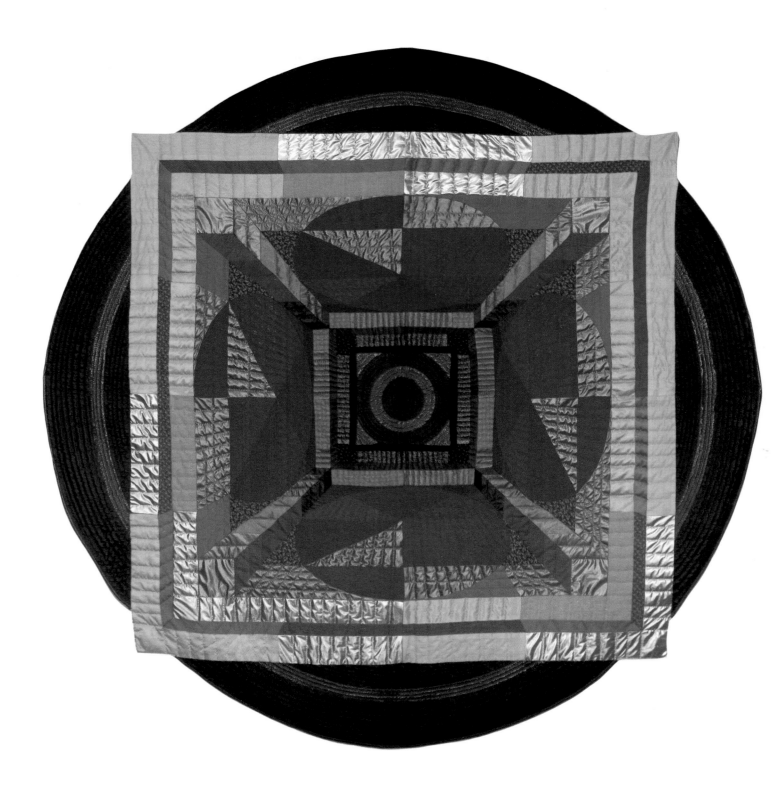

Plate 4 **TRON** courtesy of Kimberly Long Masopust

54" x 54"   1982 machine pieced, hand quilted
This quilt , using diminishing circles, was inspired by the Disney movie "Tron". Lamé fabrics cause this quilt to sparkle.

Plate 5 **C.W.II** courtesy of the artist

72" x 72" 1982 Machine pieced, hand quilted
C.W.II was created as a tool for my color class. It demonstrates how warm and cool colors react next to each other. The warm colors fighting to be in the foreground while the cool colors rest calmly in the background.

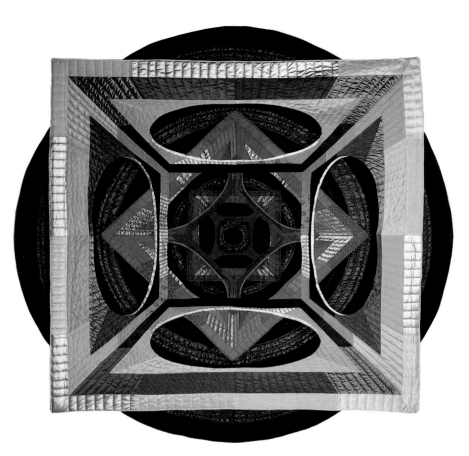

Plate 6 **SHADES OF SPACE**
courtesy of Kimberly Long Masopust

72" x 72" 1983 Machine pieced, hand quilted, bars are used to separate and hang the two quilts separately
This is a continuation of the illusion that the quilts in plate 5 and 6 are two separate quilts hanging as one.

Plate 7 **SPECTRUM** courtesy of the artist

72" x 72" 1983 Machine pieced, hand quilted,

This quilt is also two separate quilts hanging as one. One VP is used to create the dimension in the gray bars. The color wheel background intensifies the neutral foreground.

Plate 8 **UNO**   courtesy of Edward Stanton III

72" x 86" 1984 Machine pieced, hand quilted
Uno is based on an off center composition using one VP. It is the first in the ball series. The cool
background colors create a very peaceful setting upon which the fiery ball rests.

Plate 9 **SPHERES OF INFLUENCE** courtesy of Terry & MaryAnn

82" x 70"   1984 machine pieced, hand quilted
This quilt uses several of the lessons described in this book, one VP to create the floor and the wall, spheres, and shadows. The size of the spheres are different in order to create a more interesting circular composition.

Plate 10 **COSMIC SPHEROIDS** courtesy of the artist

80" x 70" 1984 machine pieced, hand quilted
The light source in this quilt comes from the center sphere. Little silver beads sewn on after the quilt was finished, enhance the feeling of spheres floating in space.

Plate 11 **ACTURUS**   courtesy of the artist

84" x 72" 1985 machine pieced, hand quilted
Having done spheres sitting on the ground and floating in space; I decided to go one step beyond, landing them on another planet: Acturus. A one VP grid was distorted to create the planet surface.

Plate 12 **THE JUGGLER** courtesy of the artist

80" x 72" 1985 Machine pieced, hand quilted
This quilt is the last in the series on spheres. A large unit is suspended in space while the spheres float
overhead.

Plate 13 **SOLAR CHAMPAGNE** courtesy of the artist

40" x 88" 1986 machine pieced, hand quilted
Solar Champagne is an exersize in transparency. A clear vase full of Christmas
ornaments inspired this design.

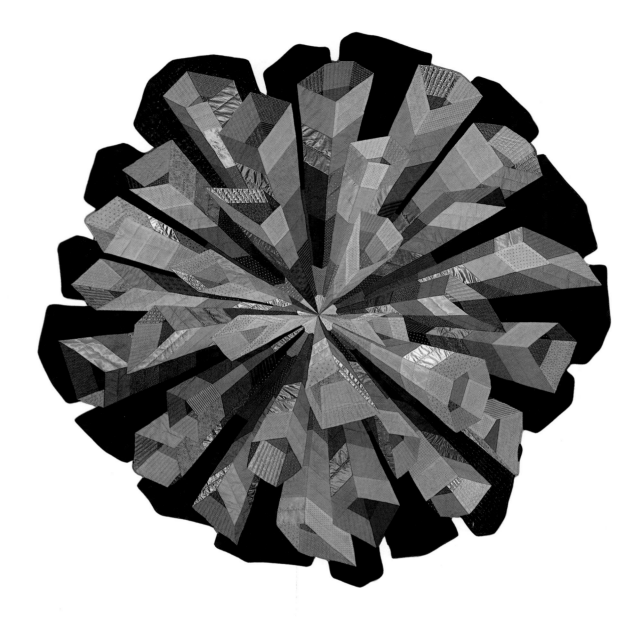

Plate 14 **ATOMIC AZALEA** courtesy of Kimberly Long Masopust

72" 1986 machine pieced, hand quilted,
This is the first quilt in the Extraterrestrial Floral Series. Each pedal of the Azalea is made up of color gradations from light to dark. The shape of each peddle leads the eye to the outside of the design, but the intensity of the center of this mandala draws you back into the center.

Plate 15 **GALACTIC GARDENIA**   courtesy of Kimberly Long Masopust

72" 1987 machine pieced, hand reverse applique, hand quilted
Another Extraterrestrial Flower reminiscent of the paintings of Victor Vasserely. The sphere is made up
of little reverse applique ovals.

Plate 16 **KURO-SHIRU** courtesy of the artist

90" x 90" 1986 machine pieced, hand reverse applique, hand quilted
In 1986 I taught in Japan and was greatly influenced by their color and simplicity in design. This quilt was a direct result of that trip. Kuro-Shiru means black and white in Japanese. Many of the colored fabrics were purchased in Japan and the circle on a square represents the Japanese flag.

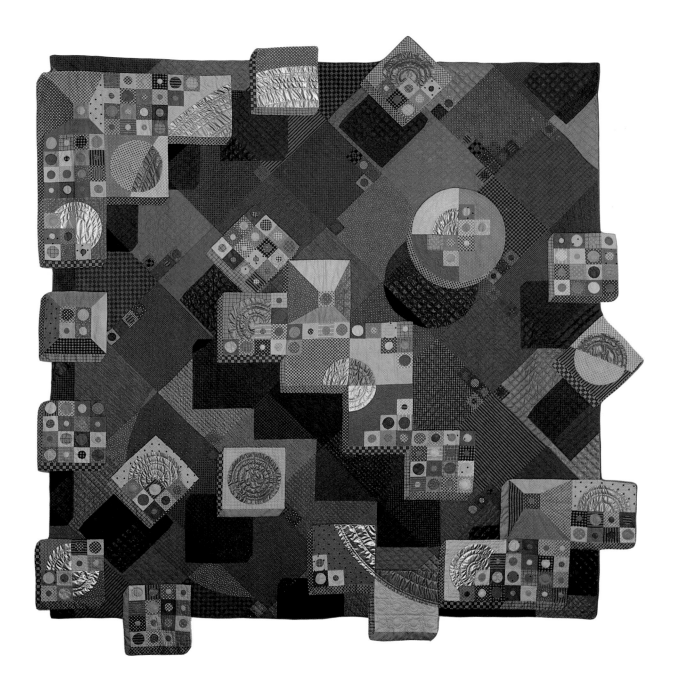

Plate 17 **CALIFORNIA COOLER** courtesy of the artist

100" x 100" 1987 machine pieced, hand reverse applique, hand quilted
California cooler it the second in the circle series. It takes the black and white version (Kuro-Shiru) a step further into color. The warm units appear to float over the cool background, enhanced by the use of shadows. It reminds me of clouds and their shadows as you fly above on a sunny day.

Plate 18 **TU-ON-TOR, TA** courtesy of the artist

84" x 62' 1988 machine pieced, hand reverse applique, hand quilted
This quilt is a direct result of a three month tour of Hawaii, New Zealand, and Australia to teach and sight
see. The three warm colored circles represent those three "islands" the small cool circle is off the coast
of "Australia" and represents the Great Barrier Reef. "TA" means Thank-you.

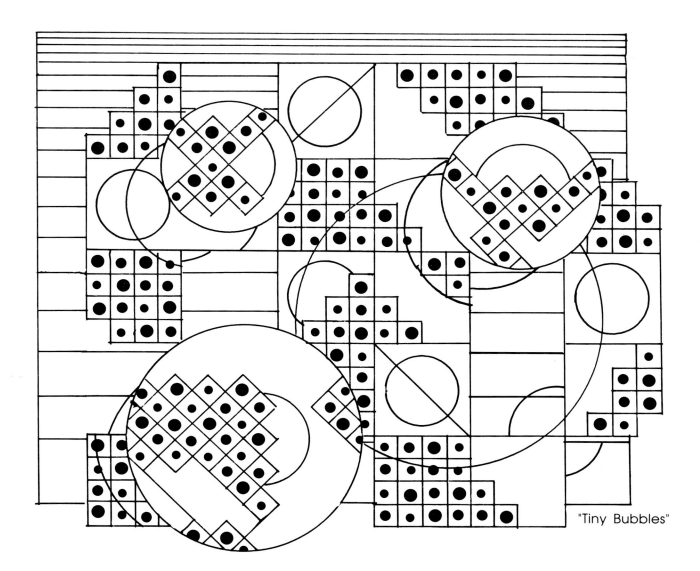

"Tiny Bubbles"

Human perception is a fascinating area of study for the simple reason that it is related to the firsthand experience of everyone. It is not something apart from life, but intimately tied in with it. Thus everyone has access to the laboratory of his own consciousness. The way may not be too easy, but at least it is personal and not remote.

Faber Birren
Creative Color

Imagine drawing a set of steps using two vanishing points. You will use the knowledge you acquired from drawing 2 pt. boxes and dividing a vertical square.

First, divide a vertical square into 16 units; also draw a small frontal view of this square. Darken the center diagonal of both the frontal and perspective square.

Darken the flats and risers of the stairs following the diagonal line.

Using a clean sheet of tracing paper, trace the steps and the two original vanishing lines and vertical lines.

Choose a second VP on the horizon line to the left of the steps. Draw vanishing lines from this VP to the two corners of the square; you are drawing a two point box on which to build the stairs. Extend the diagonal line and add another line that matches up with the top corners of the steps. Where these two lines meet will be a third VP!

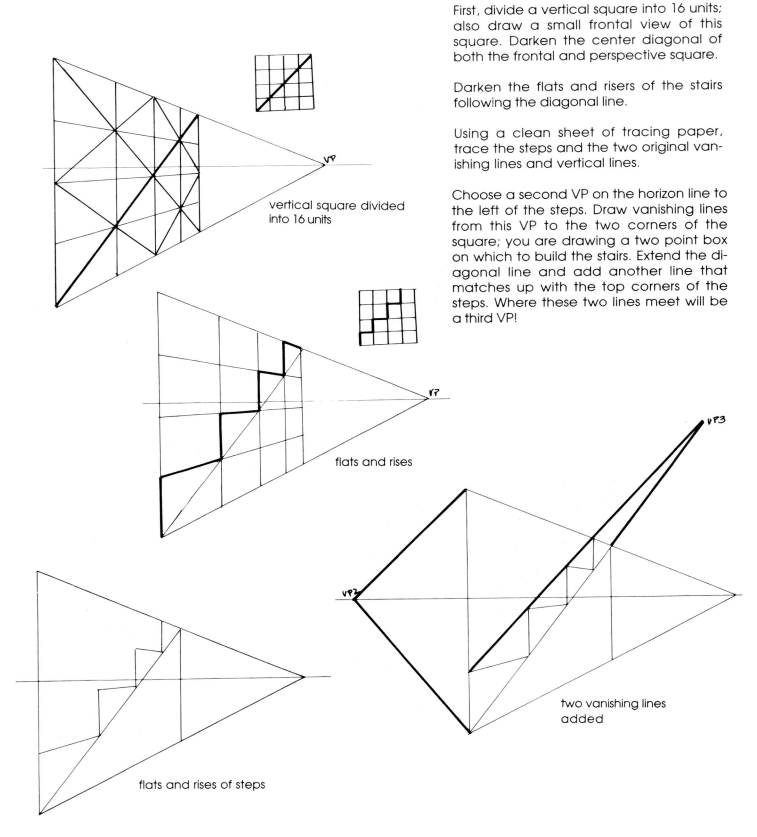

vertical square divided into 16 units

flats and rises

flats and rises of steps

two vanishing lines added

Connect each corner of the steps to the second VP with vanishing lines.

Determine the back corner of the steps and the box. Inclose them by adding a parallel line at a distance of your choice. Darken in that portion of the line between the two vanishing lines of the bottom step. From the top and bottom of the darkened portion, add two more vanishing lines going to VP3.

Starting at the top of the darkened line of the bottom step, draw a vanishing line to VP1. Darken in this line from it's beginning to where it meets the next vanishing line. Pivot the ruler and draw a vertical line parallel to the front riser. Pivot again and draw the flat to VP1, continuing up the steps. There will come a point where the flat will be hidden from view; just draw these lines lighter.

You should now be able to draw in the back of the unit, drawing from each corner to the opposite VP.

It is very easy to become confused with all these sets of vanishing lines going to three different VPs. It helps to draw the lines lightly, or to trace each successive drawing, leaving out lines that are no longer needed.

To finish the drawing, trace the steps, eliminating all the vanishing lines.

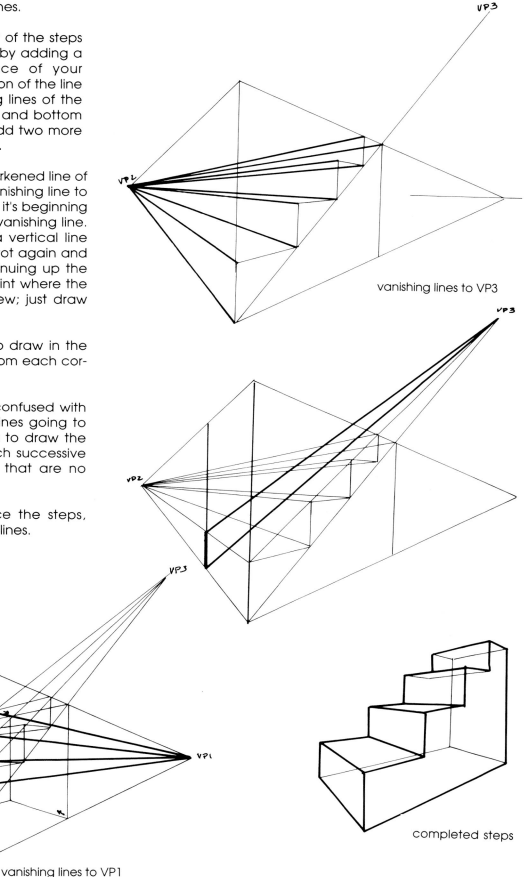

vanishing lines to VP3

vanishing lines to VP1

completed steps

Imagine a square, mentally draw a horizontal line through the center of the square. This will now be the axis. Find the center of the square by mentally drawing lines from corner to corner. Place a circle in the square, touching the sides of the square. This is a frontal view of a circle within a square. Now, rotate the square on it's axis. As one half of the square comes toward you, it becomes larger; as it goes away from you, it becomes smaller. What is happening to the circle? Is it staying a circle? It changes, becomes an ellipse, a diminishing circle. We will learn to draw this mental picture.

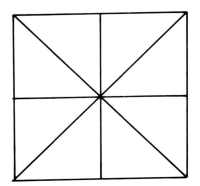

frontal view of square

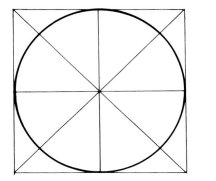

circle inscribed in square

Begin by drawing a 4" square. Use graph paper under the tracing paper to help draw the square correctly. Divide the square into eight sections, using two diagonals and two center lines. Remove the graph paper.

Inscribe a circle inside the square. Place the point of the compass where all the lines intersect. Open the compass wide enough to touch the sides of the square and draw the circle.

Add four more lines where the circle and the diagonal lines intersect. All of these lines are important and will be used as references for the diminishing circle. This is the frontal view of our square. Now that you SEE all the lines and the circle, visualize again the rotating square. Rotate this square on the horizontal axis. If you are having trouble visualizing, pick up your paper and rotate the square and notice how the circle looks. Once you have this visualized, go on drawing.

Extend the center line, the length equal to one half the square, (which is the same as the radius of the circle, or, in this case 2"). The end of this line becomes the vanishing point. Connect lines from the corners of the square to the VP. This space will be similar to a diminishing wall, or a side of a box.

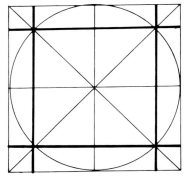

four reference lines

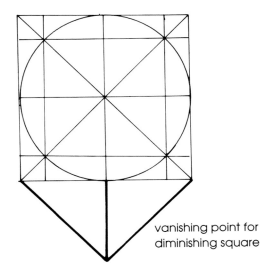

vanishing point for diminishing square

A line is needed to designate the end of the box or wall. Place this line in the middle of the triangle. See the top half of this triangle as the side of a box or wall, or as the square we have been rotating in space. This is a perspectively correct square. All of the lines in the original square need to be drawn in this square. Begin by placing diagonals from corner to corner. As we learned in drawing the diminishing wall, the center of this square is where those two lines cross. Draw a parallel line at this crossing.

Extend the inside vertical lines to the VP, (just draw the lines inside the perspective square). There are now two lines missing from the lower square that are in the top square.

The placement of those lines is determined by the crossing of the diagonal lines with the two new inside lines. Draw two lines intersecting these points, parallel to the top and bottom of the squares.

Now you have the references for the diminishing circle. Every where the circle in the first square crosses a line or touches the edge of the square, it will also cross or touch the same spot in the perspective square. There are eight reference points. Where the circle touches the edges of the square are four of these points. The other four are where the circle crosses the diagonal lines. Mark these eight spots in both the frontal square and the perspective square.

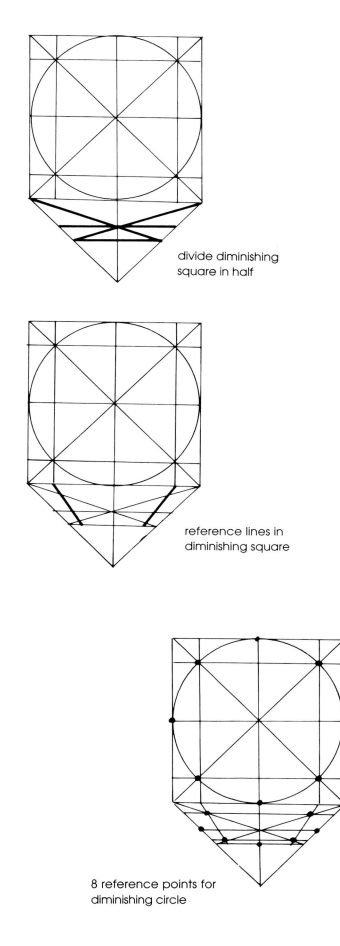

divide diminishing square in half

reference lines in diminishing square

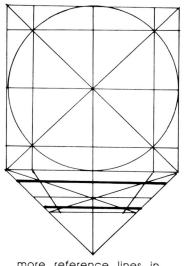

more reference lines in diminishing square.

8 reference points for diminishing circle

DIMINISHING CIRCLES..

Now let's do dot-to-dot! Connect the points with a gentle arc, free hand. The first time the circle might be a little angular but keep working to smooth and round out all the angles.

To finish the unit, a smaller square is added off the bottom of the diminishing square. Using a compass, make a circle by placing the point at the VP and opening the compass to the end of the diminishing square. Extend the corners of the diminishing square at right angles; this line should touch the edges of the circle. Extend the vanishing lines until they touch these two lines, and, at those points, enclose the square with a line at the bottom.

Repeat all the lines in the original square in the small square. Now lines run continuously through all three squares. These lines should connect at each edge, as the darkened lines show in this illustration. If these lines don't match in your drawing, then you should start again. This unit is now the repeat: original square, diminishing square, and small square.

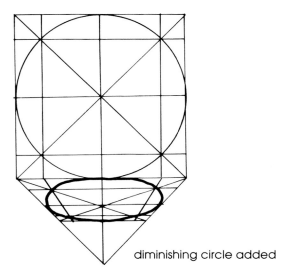

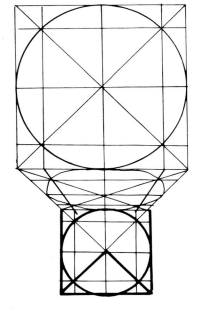

diminishing circle added

small square added off
the bottom of
diminishing square

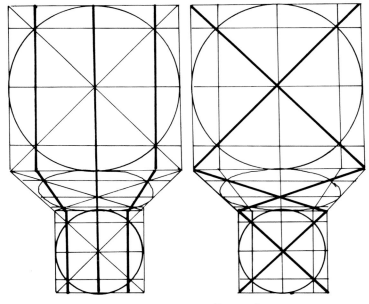

lines run continuously
through the three units

Using another piece of tracing paper, trace all the lines in these three squares. Be sure and leave enough room to the left, right and bottom to trace repeats. Once this is completed, turn the tracing paper so that the small squares match and trace the other two squares. The center of the small square is the pivot point.

If the original was drawn correctly, the edges of the diminishing square should match up. The reason they match is because the VP was exactly half the distance of the original square, which makes the angle of the vanishing lines 45 degrees. When two units are placed together they make 90 degrees, or another square. Trace the set at least twice.

If you wish to explore this design element further, you could trace four of the repeats. You can again pivot on the large square and trace the smaller two units, creating the outside corners.

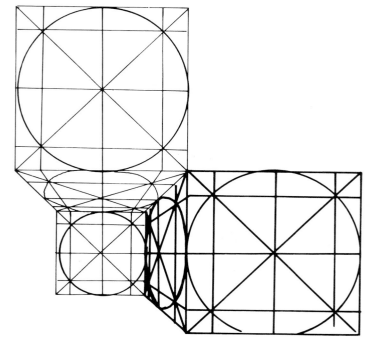

two sets combined

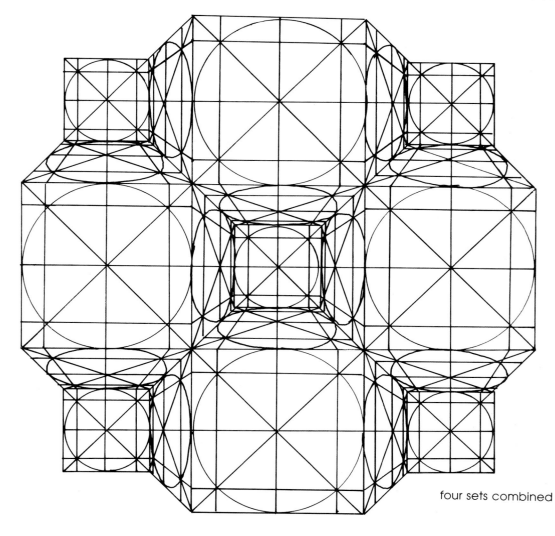

four sets combined

The idea from the previous lesson can be applied in many ways. For instance, there could be more than four repeats. In my quilt, C.W.II, (plate 5) I used six repeats of the diminishing circle.

You would work backward to make different repeats of the diminishing circle. 360 degrees equals a complete circle. Let's say we are going to make a color wheel and need six repeats to get the colors right. Divide 6 into 360 to find out how many degrees each unit must be (60 degrees). Using a protractor, draft a 60 degree angle. Measure two inches from the center on each line. Connect these to create a triangle; that distance is the length of the sides of the square needed to create a diminishing circle. Draw a square using that line as one of its sides. Use graph paper to help you get a "square" square.

Add all the lines used in the previous lesson; also add the circle. Now you can follow the rest of the steps to create the diminishing circle; trace and repeat six units to create the whole.

In C.W. II, I eliminated the frontal square and just used the circles.

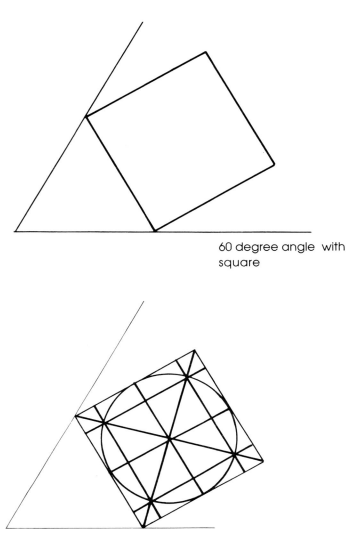

60 degree angle with square

reference lines in square

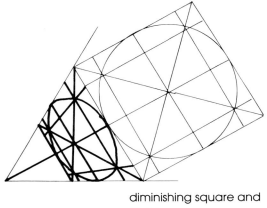

diminishing square and circle

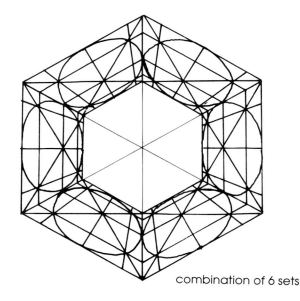

combination of 6 sets

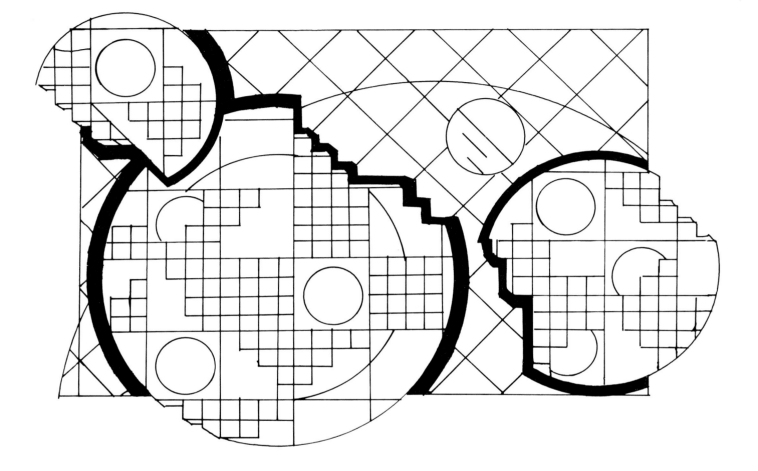

The eye carries people to different parts of the work, it is the prince of mathematics, its sciences are most certain, it has measured the heights and the dimensions of the stars, it has created architecture and perspective and divine painting

Leonardo da Vinci
Treatise on Painting

COMPOSITION

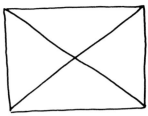

Don't place an x in the center

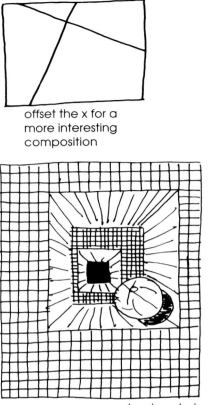

offset the x for a more interesting composition

bulls-eye

a more pleasing design with the center off set

Don't have objects directly in the corners

pull the objects within the composition

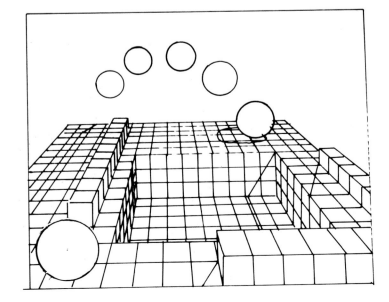

the original "Juggler" had a sphere set in the corner

Composition is the arrangement of objects or shapes. Good composition allows the viewer to travel around the piece.

When designing a new piece, I do not think of composition at first; I begin by drawing an idea, then tracing the best parts of that idea, adding (or eliminating) objects, shapes or lines until pleased with the overall effect. Admittedly, I consciously think of things I should NOT do to make a good composition. I will explain composition through my own quilts. Try some of these ideas below out on other quilts or paintings to make composition a little easier to understand.

My do's and don'ts of composition:

If an X is needed in your composition, place it off center with the ends running off the space on the sides rather than in corners. Don't divide the whole space on the diagonal with a large X. Even one diagonal line running from corner to corner breaks the composition into two equal units.

"Uno" (plate 8) was originally drawn using an X from corner to corner. This bothered me; so, I offset the X, deliberately placing each unit off center from the next. Although a less safe design, the piece is much more interesting without the bulls-eye effect.

Bring an object or line into the area of interest, making it part of the piece. Don't set an object or line directly in a corner or against the edge of the space, it will appear added as an afterthought.

Originally, "The Juggler", (plate 12) had another ball in the corner below the left wall. This awkward placement was remedied by removing the ball.

In all compositions, there is a foreground and a background. The foreground often is the center of interest. Don't make the background so overpowering that the foreground fades and seems insignificant. A foreground of bright warm colors and a background of warm pastel shades is more successful than the reverse. A pastel background allows a bright object to appear closer and in front. A background of black or very dark colors sets off a bright colored foreground.

"Galactic Gardenia" (plate 15) has a plain black flower-shaped background, to show off the bright colors of the foreground. If the background was elaborately pieced blues, for instance, the power of the sphere and cubes would diminished.

A composition of shapes or objects of all the same size can be monotonous; vary the sizes and the shapes. Color also follows this same rule. If you vary the sizes and shapes, but leave them basically the same value or color, this will result in a monotonous composition. The key is variety.

"Spheres of Influence" (plate 9) is a composition made up of balls and a light source of varied sizes and colors.

background too over powering

background should set off foreground

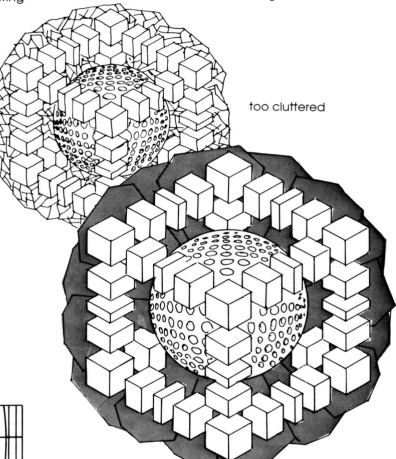

too cluttered

"Galactic Gardenia" with a black background that sets off the foreground.

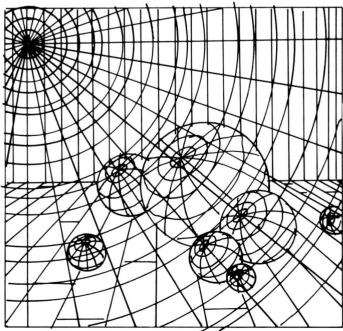

"Spheres of Infuence" with the spheres of various sizes

original with spheres all the same size

too busy

leave some areas plain to rest the eye

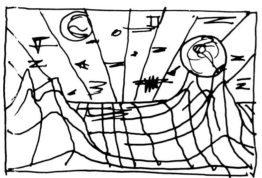

too busy

black sky inhances the foregound

It is important to have places where the eye can rest. A busy composition with many things to look at, and many colors to digest, will leave the viewer uncomfortable. Give variety to the spaces. Create some busy spaces and some quiet backgrounds, or design a shape for the eye to settle on for a moment.

"Acturus" (plate 11) is a quiet planet somewhere in space. If the black sky was made up of lots of little fabric pieces representing stars and space-things, the quilt would not be a peaceful fantasy. The choice of a solid sky keeps the viewers interest on the landscape and not the sky.

In any composition, there is positive and negative space. The positive space is the object or shape of the theme. The negative space is the space around the object. Both spaces are important. A piece with too much negative space around the object will feel incomplete; or, it may give the feeling of loneliness, (objects together but not interacting). Too little negative space will appear jumbled or crowded. A balance is needed between the two. Also, the negative space should be interesting no matter what the subject of the positive space. Trace the negative spaces; look at the negative spaces traced as a composition: Is it pleasing? Some negative shapes may be awkward, change these by shifting the positive objects.

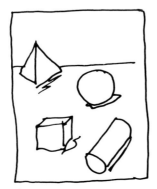

too much negative space

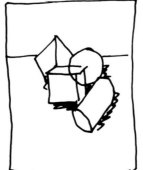

objects too tightly grouped

a more pleasing relationship between negative and positive space.

Circular composition keeps your eye moving around and around. Place the point or object of interest in an off center position to help the flow and interest of the composition. Don't place the center of interest directly in the center of the space, this bulls-eye effect doesn't allow the eye to travel comfortably without always ending right in the center.

In "Threshold of a Dream" (plate 3) the eye begins at the end of the hall; the center of interest is not in the center of the piece. The eye goes to the right edge, then up or down, and back to the center (off center), going around and around with the circles in the wall, but always back to the center because of the lamé, only to be thrown back to the right again and again.

bulls-eye effect

a more interesting off center composition

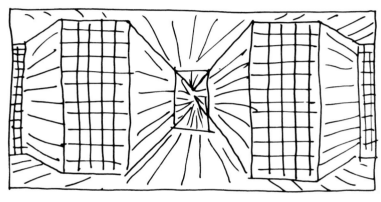
original idea for "Threshold of a Dream"

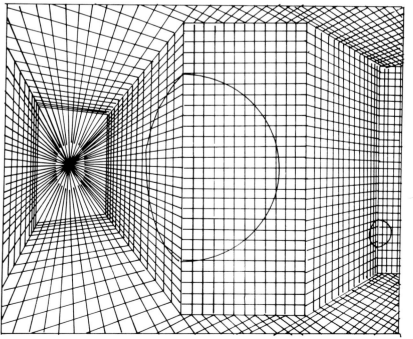
"Threshold of a Dream"

The use of lights and darks is also important to consider. Place the darks unevenly throughout the piece. Placing them evenly will give a checkerboard effect, and, unless you want a checkerboard, you could be turning a good composition into a patchwork feeling. Group lights and darks together to help create a light source with a dramatic dark area. Shadows closer to the light source are lighter than shadows further away. Group objects casting shadows together, rather than set out like chessmen.

The optical illusion of space between layers or objects helps a composition; in "Kiro-Shiru" (plate 16) and "California Cooler" (plate 17), the foreground and background are separated by space. Kiru has three layers: the squares or boxes in front, a middle layer of flat black and white shapes, and a background of lighter shades of grays. California Cooler takes this idea one step further, and blatantly adds definite shadows of the warm colored units floating high above the cool background.

even spacing of dark areas create a checker board effect

group lights and darks

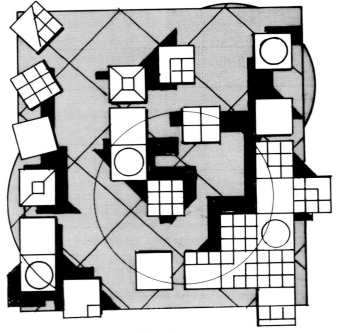

Kiro-Shiru

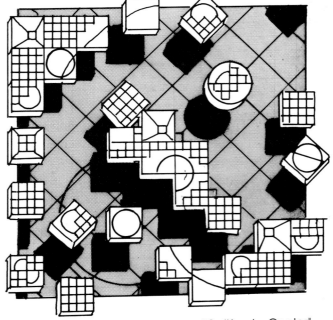

"California Cooler"

Direct the viewer to your quilt. Strong directional lines will lead the eye in one direction. Make sure that is the direction you want the viewer to follow. If a line directs them outside of the space, they may be lead away, off to view other pieces. If you lead them out of the quilt, another strong object, or directional line, can pull the viewer back into the space.

There are very strong directional lines in "The Juggler" (plate 12). The viewer enters the quilt on the left side, through the dark shadow; their eye follows the warm colored wall up, then follows the floating balls down onto the cool surface of the floating deck. Their eye continues along the golden wall right off the quilt; but, the golden wall at the bottom pulls them back onto the surface because it is bright and demands their return. Then continuing on back to the warm wall on the left and up and around the piece again.

Many objects in a single design should belong together on the same plane. The objects need to look as if they are in the same area. Lots of objects together with none touching will appear floating in space with no regard for each other. The solution is to move the objects so some are overlapping, as if one is in front of the other.

We become more knowledgeable in any field by studying it. That knowledge helps to define what is acceptable or pleasing to us as individuals. Study prize winning quilts; look through art books; go to museums. If a painting or a quilt doesn't please you in the overall effect, try to find something in it that does: a combination of lines, color choice in a certain area, fabric combinations, textures, anything. There has got to be something pleasing in everything you see, sometimes it's a great challenge to find. Also, study the lines of the composition; try to decide why a composition does or doesn't work. The more you observe the more knowledgeable you will become.

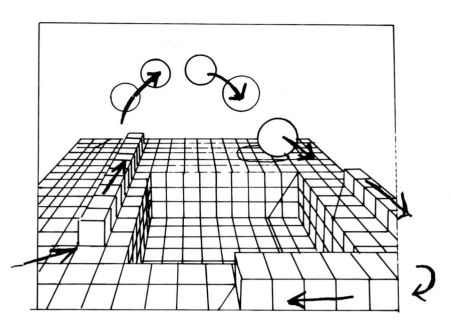

strong directional lines lead the viewer through the piece

too much space between objects

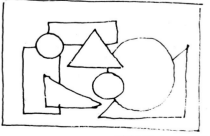

objects brought together on the same plane

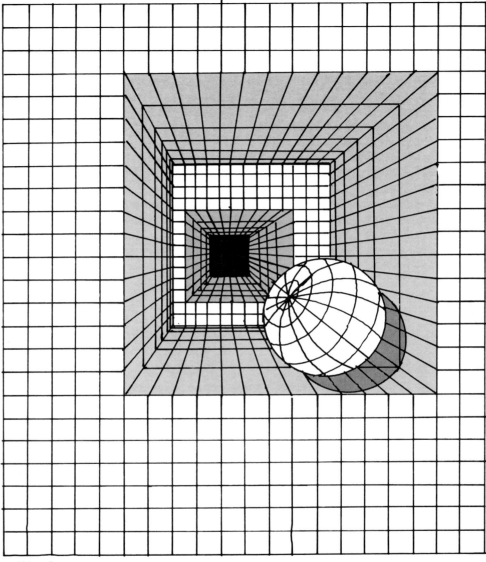

"Uno"

What we sometimes wrongly regard as talent is in fact a gradual, discrete and continual self-training of interested children at play with their imaginations. This way of playing is common to the great majority of children, and while some of them abandon it for other interests, those who persist through the later years of adolescence are potential creative artists.

Radu Vero
Understanding Perspective

Color! There are so many things that can be said and felt about color. I personally choose my colors from an emotional reaction to my design and the fabrics in front of me. I think too much studying of color can stifle one's natural ability, but, some background of color is necessary to have the confidence to create. With this in mind, I have included here the points on color that I relate to fibre artists, or quilt artists. Try some of the exercises; if nothing else, they can be made into a nice pillow for Aunt Martha.

A bit of information on the color wheel:

Primary colors: Red, Yellow, Blue. From these all colors can be made.

Secondary colors: Orange, Green, Purple or Violet. Colors that are mixed from the primaries.

The combination of primary and secondary colors will be referred to as "the big 6"

Complimentary color sets: Red - Green, Orange - Blue, Yellow - Purple. Colors that are opposite on the color wheel.

Warm Colors: Red, Orange, Yellow. Colors that appear in fire.

Cool Colors: Green, Blue, Purple. Colors that appear in water.

Tints: Pink, Peach, Lavender. Colors with white added to them.(Pastels)

Shades: Brown, Olive, Navy. Colors with black added.

Tones: Tan, Dusty Pink. Colors with black and white added.(Dusty colors)

Saturation: The amount of pure color in a color. Red has a high saturation, while pink has a low saturation.

Value: How light or dark a color is. White has a high value, while black has a low value.

EXERCISE: Using circles or squares of your own collection, put together a color wheel using the primary and secondary colors; then add the intermediate colors, (those colors created by mixing two adjacent colors from the big 6). Lastly, add white and black to the big 6.

EXERCISE: Chose any piece of fabric from your collection. Use as many of the above terms to explain its color. Example: Red: warm, high saturation, primary. Light brown: warm, tone, low saturation.

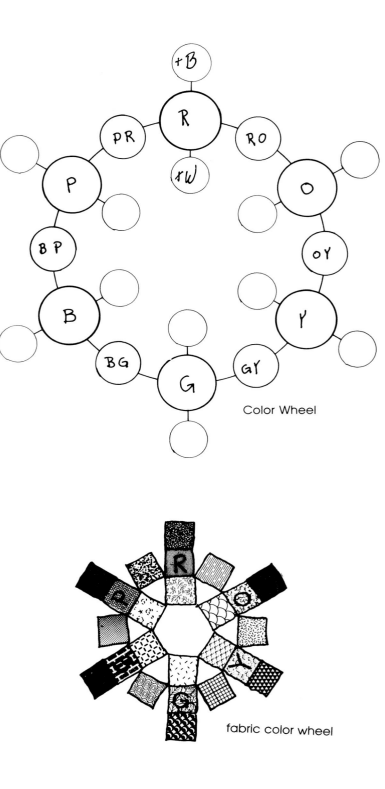

Color Wheel

fabric color wheel

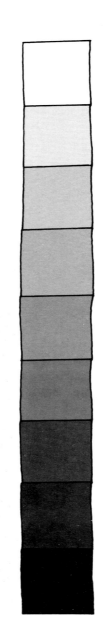

Tints:
white added to color

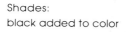

Shades:
black added to color

A complete color run from
white to black

Color Runs :

To change the value of a color, white or black is added. When working with paints this is done by combining pigments. When working with fabrics, this is done by choice of already colored samples.

EXERCISE: Chose one of the big six colors (primary and secondary colors). Imagine this is a glob of paint on your palate. Mix a touch of white paint to this color. What color would your get? Try and find that color in your fabric collection. Now imagine mixing a touch of white to this second color. What color would you now have? Find that color in your collection. Add white to that color; continue this process until you have a very high value, or white itself. These are all tints.

Now, let's add black to our original color to get the shades. Imagine what this color would look like with a bit of black included. Find that color in your collection. Continue adding black until the last choice is black. This is a color run from a high value, white, through pure color, to the lowest value, black.

When you have finished this experiment, take a reducing tool and view the color run. Does your eye run evenly through the colors? If you tend to notice one color above the others, it may be wrong. There are various reasons a piece of fabric may stand out. It could be that it has a mixture of colors in it; a red could have too much blue (rather than black) in it to make it darker, and it would stand out as a cool red. A color may have black as well as white added to it, and that would make it too dark for the white side and too light for the black side.

Another problem could be in the actual print of fabric. A piece of fabric with too many colors in it is confusing. A piece of fabric should look like one color no matter how many actual colors it contains. The smaller the print the easier it is for the eye to blend the colors and see one dominate color. If the actual print is too large, the eye will see all the colors as separate entities and the color run will not be smooth. I use color runs in my quilts to help with the dimension. The darkest side of the run being used for shadows, while the lightest side creates the effect of light shining on an object.

Size:

Colors of close value tend to group themselves. In these two squares, three values are used: white, gray and black. Both examples are exactly the same size, but the placement of the values causes the eye to insist they are not. In the first illustration, the white center looks smaller than the black center. This is because the gray tends to group with the black, making the black and gray combinations appear larger; thus, the white areas appear smaller. This phenomena controls the weight or size of shapes. When working on a quilt, it is good to keep in mind how colors will group, giving greater weight to one shape or section.

Order:

There is a natural order to color, from light to dark, or from one color to the next around the color wheel. The choice of the order of black, gray and white in the first set of squares is that of a natural order. In the following four squares, the order is changed and causes a sense of discord in the squares. This is helpful to keep in mind; if a comfortable natural composition is desired, it would be helpful to keep colors in a natural order.

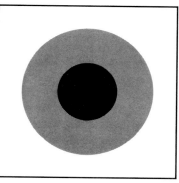

colors of close value group
together, appearing larger

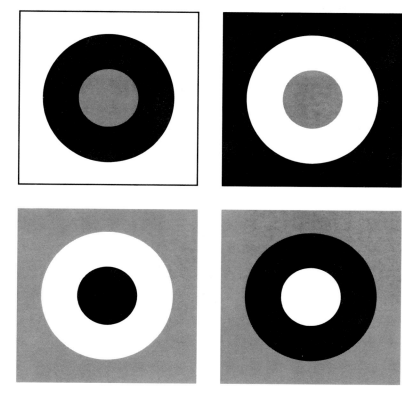

unnatural order of black,
gray and white, causing
discord

gradations of gray placed together create a fluting effect.

Gray Scale:

A gray scale is another helpful tool. It can be used to measure the value of any given color scale.

EXERCISE: Chose 10 gray fabrics from your collection and place them in order from white to black. Be sure your grays are all a neutral gray. You will discover there can be many other colors in any given gray besides black and white. You could have a warm gray, one in which a touch of red can be seen. Or, you could have a cool gray; a blue or green has been included. The reducing tool will help find these culprits and eliminate them so only the neutral grays remain. Paste or sew this gray run together to be used in a later exercise.

When strips of gray values are placed next to each other in a natural order, a different kind of phenomena occurs. As one value touches the darker value, it appears lighter on the edge, creating a fluting effect .

Lighting:

Colors appear to change depending on the amount of light they receive. Actually, the colors don't change at all; what the eye perceives changes depending upon the amount of available light. The middle values tend to blend together when there is a small amount of light. These values will change toward the darker colors.

EXERCISE: Take your gray run into a darkened room and see how many of the gradations you can distinguish. Do the same thing with your color run. While choosing colors for a quilt, you might decide not to use so many middle values since they tend to blend together under minimal light. Take these same gray and color runs and place them under a bright light and see how the colors look.

Simultaneous Contrast:

Colors change depending upon which colors are placed together. They can change in brightness or they can change in what color you actually see.

If two identical gray circles are placed on a white square and a black square, the brightness of the grays will change. The gray on the white square will appear a shade or two darker than the actual color; the circle on the black square will appear a shade or two lighter. The difference in the background value will cause the gray circle to accent the brightness of the white and the depth of the black

EXERCISE: Try this same theory on colored fabrics. Cut two identical red circles. Place one circle on a square of it's compliment, green, and one red circle on it's adjacent color, orange. What happens to the red circle? The red circle with the orange fabric appears deeper. The colors are adjacent to one another on the color wheel, so they draw strength from each other. The red circle on it's compliment, appears brighter; compliments intensify each other.

simultaneous contrast

Afterimage:

In simultaneous contrast of colors, an afterimage is apparent. Stare at the black circle intensely for a moment or two; then, switch your eyes to the small black circle. What do you now see? You will see the compliment color as an afterimage to the first circle. White and black are complimentary colors.

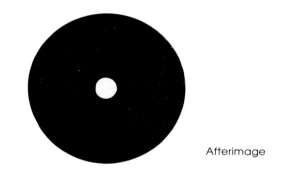

Afterimage

EXERCISE: Cut a shape out of colored fabric and place it on a white surface. Stare at the shape for a moment; then, stare at the white surface. What do you see? The afterimage should be the opposite color, the original color's complimentary color. For instance, if the original color is yellow, then the afterimage would be purple. The reason for this afterimage is, staring at one color long enough, your eye fatigues; when you look away, the part of the eye used to see the original color will rest and the opposite color will take it's place.

Afterimage

complimentarily colors will cause a vibration

complimentary colors placed together in small amounts create mud.

Afterimage can change the overall color of a color scheme. Look at the large black and white squares; they vibrate. Black and white are complimentary colors. A vibration sets up from the afterimage of each square. When we place black and white colors in a smaller area, strips, the colors will blend causing a gray appearance. Thus size is important in color choices.

EXERCISE: Try this theory with colored fabric. First, use a set of complimentary colors and see what happens. When yellow and purple are placed together, the same effect as the black and white squares will be apparent. Because purple and yellow are complimentary, they will vibrate. The afterimage of yellow is purple and purple is yellow; so, you will see the opposite color when looking at each square. Hence, the vibration between each square. If you look intently at the unit for a moment , then look away at a white surface, you will see the same unit in reverse.

Place 1/2" strips of purple and yellow together. Stand back and look at this example through a reducing tool. What is the effect:? In paint, when complimentary colors are mixed, a muddy color results. Here too, when we stand back far enough to allow our eyes to mix the two complimentary colors, we get mud.

Try two colors that are adjacent to each other on the color wheel, for example green and blue. When adjacent colors are placed together, a different effect is caused by the afterimage. The afterimage of the green squares is red, it's complimentary color. Thus, the blue squares will appear to have a slightly purple appearance. Similarly, the afterimage of blue is orange, giving the green the illusion of yellow added. This is why the fabric you choose at the store doesn't always work placed next to other fabrics. Now, if you take the same two colors and make 1/2" wide strips side by side, a cool blue-green surface will appear, unlike the muddy or gray surface of the first two exercise.

Opposite colors are best used in larger areas; when used in small areas in combination they will look muddy, while adjacent colors work well in small units.

Complimentary Colors:

Complimentary colors intensify each other, making them a natural choice for accents. In a purple dominated color scheme, yellow as an accent will brighten the scheme. This may appear a little too harsh. A better choice might be to use the split-compliments, those colors on either side of the compliment. The purple color scheme could use yellow-orange or yellow-green as the accent for a more refined contrast.

Warm and Cool Colors:

Warm colors come forward and cool colors recede. Imagine two equal squares; one square is brilliant red, and one square is brilliant blue. These two squares are equal distance from the eye. Notice the visual difference between them.

Red, orange, and yellow are related to the colors of fire and are called warm colors. Green, blue, and purple relate to ice colors and are called cool colors. The eye focuses differently on the two colors. Warm colors appear closer and, therefore, larger; and cool colors recede and seem smaller.

In chosing color to enhance a perspective drawing, warmer colors are logical for objects in the foreground (those you wish to appear in front of, or on top of another.) Similarly, cool colors work nicely as background. This doesn't mean that you couldn't reverse the colors, it is just easier to read what your eye sees naturally.

Atmosphere:

Close colors are more intense, while remote ones are softer and faded. This has to do with atmosphere; (the photons within the air) objects appear lighter the further away they get. Look at a mountain range; as the mountains recede they appear to lighten and soften.

To demonstrate this idea of atmosphere, picture the circles fading from black to white as they recede. Because of the photons, white will never appear as pure white; it will always be a light gray.

Contrasts between colors change the mood of the piece. If the colors are bright and highly contrasting, the piece will be emotionally charged, energetic. In opposition, if the colors are very subtle and pale, the emotional reaction will be one of piece and tranquility.

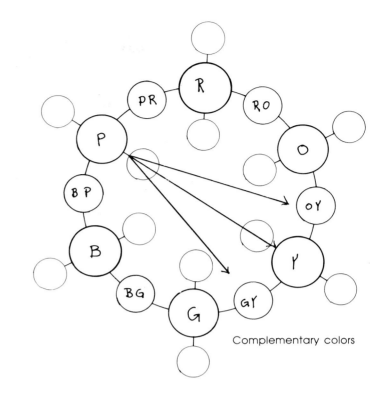

Complementary colors

atmosphere causes colors to soften

Transparency:

Transparency is the effect of being able to look through one color to another. These two circles are opaque, and lying one behind the other. In the next example, a transparent effect is created by using different shades of gray. The overlap of two grays creates a third gray, a combination of the two hues.

EXERCISE: Try transparency with colors. Choose a few simple colors at first; use a red and yellow circle. Where they overlap will be orange. Red + Yellow = Orange. Blue and green will cause the overlap to be turquoise. A more difficult combination in fabric would be mixing complimentary colors. Red and green would cause the transparency to appear as a combination of those two colors, which would result in a brown of red and green. When working with fabrics, some pieces will have both colors in them; for example, a green background with red flowers. If the print is small enough, the eye will blend the colors to get the needed transparency.

Space and distance cause colors to fade or blend. Notice the two samples. In the first set, the circle is near and the background appears to be far away. In the second set, the fine strips of the print bring the background fabric directly behind the circles; the stripes cause the eye to notice the background. When working on a quilt, be sure not to use large bold stripes or prints for background unless you want the background to appear on the same plane as the foreground.

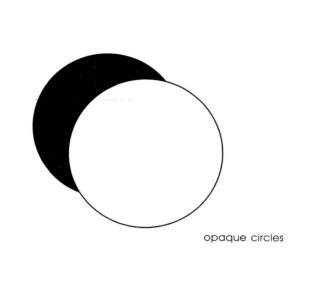

opaque circles

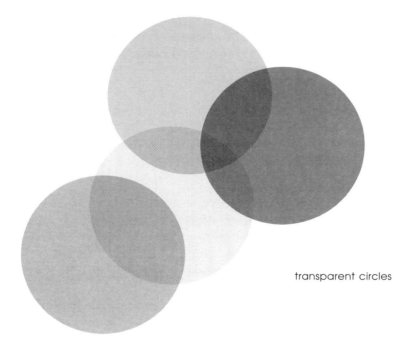

transparent circles

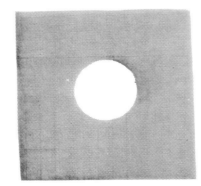

background fabrics

Color & Composition

In traditional quilts and mandala quilts, the composition is symmetrical because it consists of repeating units. To add more interest to these compositions, I choose not to use identical color choices in each set. The value of the color may be the same to keep the continuity of the pattern, but the actual fabric can be different (solid, large print, or small print.) Pink cotton could be used in one set, a pink print in another, and a pink lame in a third. In "Tron" and CWII" and "Melanie's Rose", the repeats or sets are the same but there are subtle color changes within each repeat; either a change of fabric pattern or a change in fiber content. If each repeat was the same there would be no need to view each section separately. Different fabrics throughout allow the viewer to enjoy the whole, and each unit alone.

Melanie's Rose

It is important to know the basics of color; but too many people depend on, and are often intimidated, by theory when chosing colors. My approach to color is spontaneity; I do not color in my drawings. I decide first where the cools and the warms will go; I visualize this, then begin by cutting out the pieces and pinning them to the wall. I try not to think, "Is this the right color for this piece? Will this piece go with it? What color will I put in the far corner if I put this one here? "There are just too many questions! All these questions do is confuse one and stop the creative flow. Instead, I pin up the first piece, then go with my first choice for the next piece without concern for the following pieces. My choices are determined by what is already decided, not by what will make the next decision easy. I call this "going with the flow", the creative flow.

I have watched people agonize over choices as if each decision is final. Nothing is set in stone; we are working with fabric, and any decision can be changed. I find it easiest to continue cutting and pinning until there is a good amount pinned up, THEN sit back and decide if the colors are going in a good direction, not necessarily the direction you thought they would go but a good one.

This is a more emotional way of working with color. Rather than reading in a book what color should be put next to what color, you are responding with what feels good to **you**.

Now you have a wonderful drawing that you want to bring to life as a quilt! How do you get from a piece of tracing paper to a full blown quilt? Enlarge it!

There are two ways to enlarge; One is by figuring the ratio, the other by figuring the proportion. The results of either method will be the same.

Ratio: Measure your drawing; let's say its 6" x 8". Decide how big you want the finished quilt to be. Let's assume you want it to be 80" wide. Divide the width of the drawing (8") into the width of the quilt (80"). 80" divided by 8" gives you a ratio of 10, simple! Now every measurement in the drawing will be multiplied by 10 to give how big it will be in the enlargement. If a line is 1" in the drawing it would be 10" in the enlargement. If a line was 3/4" in the drawing it would be 7 1/2"; everything multiplied by 10. This gets a little more complicated if your ratio isn't an easy number like 10. Say your ratio was 9 3/8". That would be a little more difficult to multiply. Round your ratio up or down to make it easy on yourself. I would round this to a ratio of 9 1/2" or 10".

Proportional scale: There are two wheels on a proportional scale. A large white one, and a small tan one. The tan wheel in the center is always the size of the drawing. The wheel on the outside is the size of the enlargement. Let's figure how to enlarge your design using the same figures as before. Find the width of the drawing (8") on the small wheel, and the width of the quilt on the large wheel. Turn the wheels so these two figures match. There is a small window in the center wheel; this window tells you what percentage the drawing is to the finished quilt, (10% in this case). This % is not that important in our use. The figures on the outside of the two wheels are the ones we need to deal with. Once the two original figures are set, the wheel is not moved again. Tape the wheels to keep them in place. Find the drawing measurement on the inside wheel and the outer wheel will tell you what the enlarged measurement will be. If a measurement on the drawing is 3/4 of an inch, it would be 7 1/2 on the enlargement. Find 3/4 on the center wheel and look to the outer wheel to find the enlargement, 7 1/2.

Now you have the knowledge to make your templates by enlarging your drawing.

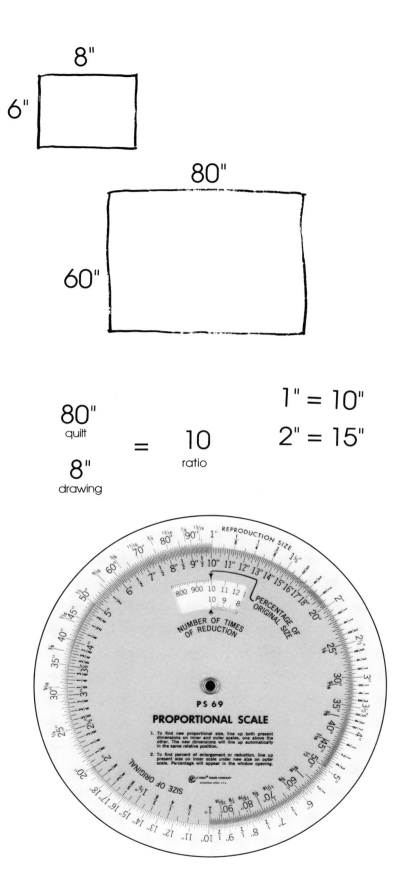

$$1" = 10"$$
$$2" = 15"$$

$$\frac{80" \text{ quilt}}{8" \text{ drawing}} = 10 \text{ ratio}$$

proportional scale

I make my templates out of a medium weight matt board ("railroad board".) Choose a weight easy to cut with scissors but heavy enough to mark around (4 ply works best). You need an area of matt board as large as your quilt. You will have to tape several sheets together, depending on the finished size of your quilt. Lay the sheets of matt board on the floor, shiny side up. Using masking tape, tape all of the seams so you have one large sheet. Turn the whole thing over and you have the surface upon which to draw your quilt.

Pick a starting point from one edge of your drawing; it can be any edge. Using the ratio or the proportional scale, begin by measuring a line or distance on your drawing and transferring it to the railroad board. Continue on in this manner until your entire quilt is drawn on the matt board. I do this sitting on the floor in the middle of it all. Play some good non-distracting music, and take it one step at a time; or more appropriately, one line at a time. If you get frustrated take a brake and come back later. Remember, this is supposed to be fun!

Trim any excess away, and you have all of your templates! Before cutting these templates apart you will need to add reference marks. Reference marks help to align fabric pieces so everything will fit and lie flat. They are especially important when working with curves. Make little pencil marks where seams will need to meet. If there is a particularly long seam a few marks will help assure accuracy. I mark curves every inch or so to align the pieces when easing in fullness. These marks are similar to marks used in garment making. Only one line is used for a reference mark in quilting and these marks are never cut into the fabric; they are transferred with pencil.

Cut the marked matt board into individual templates, and pin them to your pin up wall in order, until your whole quilt pattern is upon the wall. Now you are ready to cut out fabrics and bring life to your quilt.

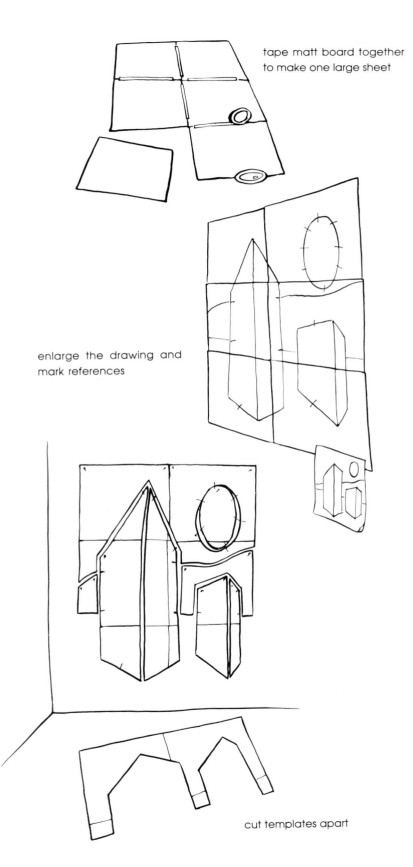

tape matt board together to make one large sheet

enlarge the drawing and mark references

cut templates apart

There are several ways to use templates when making a quilt. One school of thought is to add the seam allowance to each template. When you mark around the template you are marking your cutting line. Another way is to make two templates, one being the sewing line, the other being the cutting line. With this method you have to mark each piece twice.

I prefer a third method; I mark my sewing line onto the back of the fabric, then eyeball cutting 1/4" bigger on all sides. I find this to be more accurate and less time consuming, especially when working with curves or corners. The templates you have drawn on the large sheets of railroad board are all you need.

Once you have an idea for the colors you wish to use, begin by cutting out some fabric. Press each piece before you mark it. Lay the fabric upside down on the cutting surface and mark the seam line and reference points using your templates. Then cut the piece out approximately 1/4" bigger all the way around. It is not terribly important to cut this exactly, because you will follow the sewing line not the cut edge.

Now take the template and the cut fabric and pin them to the pin-up wall with the template behind the fabric. This way if you want to change a piece of fabric the template is right there. Continue cutting and pinning until it is all up. Stop every now and then to view your work through some sort of reducing tool to see how things are coming along. When you are completely through cutting and pinning sit back and study your work. Look through the reducing tool. If at this time anything seems out of place change it. Change things until you are satisfied. When satisfied, you are ready to sew.

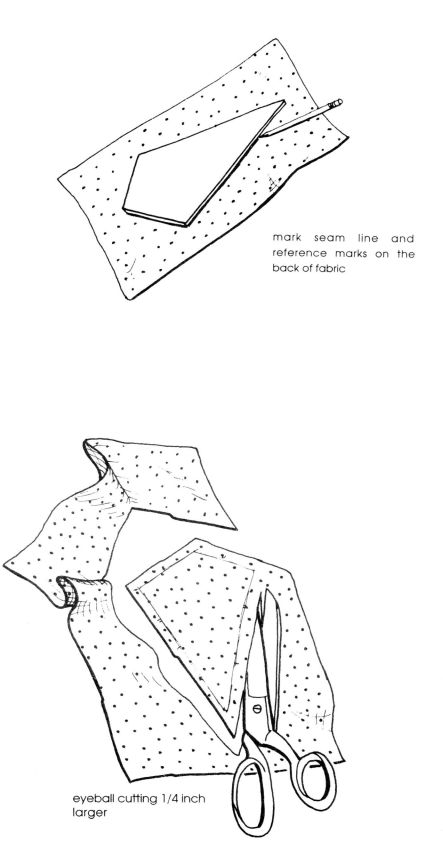

mark seam line and reference marks on the back of fabric

eyeball cutting 1/4 inch larger

Only a couple of techniques are needed to piece any quilt together. They are: straight seams and curved seams. All seams consist of one or both of these two techniques.

Straight Seam: This technique consists of pinning straight seams together, matching all reference marks and sewing, running the needle straight down the seam line. Corners are sewn using straight seams. In this example, a zigzag seam is used to illustrate my point. This is not to be considered one zigzag seam; it is a combination of three straight seams. First, sew a straight seam from end to corner, stopping and back stitching exactly at the corner. Remove the fabric from the machine; clip the inside corner right up to the seam line. Turn the fabric and straighten so there is no fabric inside the sewing line. Return to the machine and position the fabric with the needle at the corner, and sew a straight seam along the sewing line to the next corner. Again, remove the fabric from the machine and clip.

Curved Seam: This technique consists of pinning curved pieces together, matching reference marks and sewing just as in the straight seam. Pin all reference marks and sewing lines so that they match. Place the inside curve up, so you can watch to insure no tucks are sewn into the seam. The actual stitching is straight on the sewing line, while you ease the curve smoothly along to meet the needle.

I prefer to press all of my seams open. This creates a smoother seam line and makes it easier to quilt through less layers.

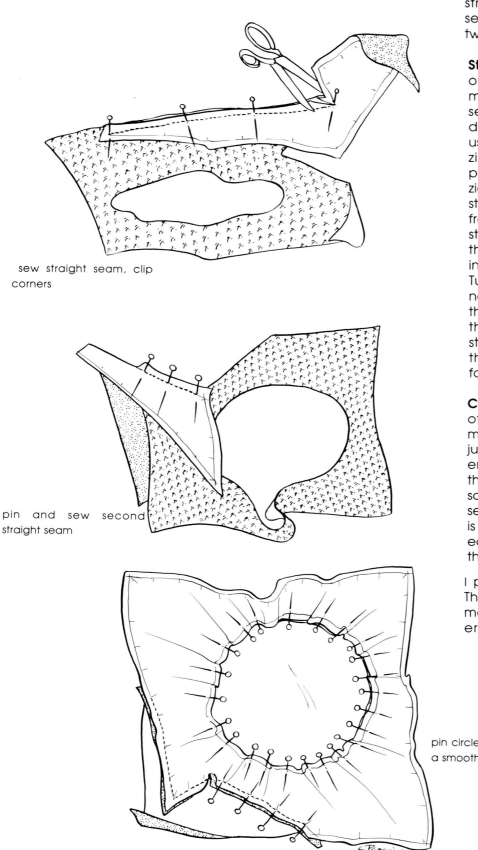

sew straight seam, clip corners

pin and sew second straight seam

pin circles closely to insure a smooth curve

C. Pasquini

I have asked my photographer, Lindsay Olsen to write a little on the photographing of quilts. He has taken the photographs of my quilts for over ten years. He has some very good pointers for you:

Let's assume you aren't a photographer, you don't even own a 35mm S.L.R. camera, but you want nice pictures of your quilts. Pin your quilt on a blank wall at eye level. Look thru your instamatic camera and fill the frame about 85% with the quilt. Take one photo with a flash and one without, this will give you a choice of exposures.

Now let's say you or a friend have a 35mm S.L.R. camera. First don't be intimidated, if you can make a quilt you can certainly operate a camera! First try the above method inside your home. Then try taking your quilt outside, preferable on a bright overcast day. Pin you quilt against a clean wall, compose your quilt in the viewfinder, remember the quilt should fill 85% of the frame, put your camera on a tripod for support, then take three different photos of each quilt. One at what the light meter says (or automatic), then take one 2 stops over-exposed, or +2 on your automatic camera, then take one more 2 stops under-exposed, or -2 on the auto dial. This technique is called "bracketing", it's what the pro's do to absolutely guarantee a perfect exposure.

When you get your slides back, pick the best of the three to show. If you'd like more consistent "controlled" light buy 2 light stands (about $35.00 at your local camera store) or you could make some using clamp lights from the hardware store. Get some light bulbs, 100 watt is good, and buy TUNGSTON film from your camera store. Set up your lights at a 45 degree angle to the quilt and about ten feet away from it both at mid-level. With your camera on a tripod make your exposures, don't forget to bracket!

outside photography on the side of a building

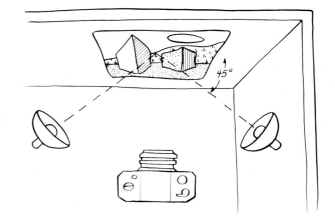

inside photography with home made lights

Bibliography ......

Vero, Radu, *Understanding Perspective,* Van Nostrand Reinhold Company 1980

Coulin, Claudius, *Step-By-Step Perspective Drawing,* Van Nostrand Reinhold Company 1982

Fabri, Ralph, *Artist's Guide to Composition,* Watson-Guptill Publications 1986

Birren, Faber, *Color Perception In Art, Principles Of Color, Creative Color,* Van Nostrand Reinhold Company

Chevreul, M.E., *The Principles of Harmony and Contrast of Colors,* Van Nostrand Reinhold Company 1967

Franck, Rederick, *The Zen of Seeing,* Vintage Books 1973

Deken, Joseph, *Computer Images, State of the Art,* Stewart, Tabori & Chang 1983

Learning from books and teachers is like traveling by carriage, so we are told in the Veda. The thought goes on, "But the carriage will service only while one is on the highroad, he who reaches the end of the highroad will leave the carriage and walk afoot"

Johannes Itten
The Art of Color